BY AIR MAIL
PAR AVION

Scale

0 100 200 300
Miles

SINKIANG

INDIA
1 Calcutta   4 Hyderabad
2 Bombay   5 Lahore
3 Madras   6 Delhi
★ New Delhi

AFGHANISTAN
★ Kabul   = Khyber Pass

NEPAL   BHUTAN
★ Katmandu   ★ Punaka

SINKIANG

AFGHANISTAN

Oxus River

Kabul

Kandahar

Helmund R.

Baluchistan

Indus

HIMALAYAS

Indus R.

TIBET

Brahmaputra

NEPAL

Mt. Everest

BHUTAN

Brahmaputra

5

6

Agra

Jumna

Ganges

Benares

Allahabad

Ganges

BURMA

I N D I A

Narbada

Gulf of Cambay

GOLD

4

GOA

1

Arabian Sea

Bay of Bengal

Mysore

3

CEYLON

Colombo

Adam's Peak

Indian Ocean

Houseboat on the Ganges
&
A Room in Kathmandu

Letters from India + Nepal
1966-1972

Marilyn Stablein

All of the photographs, collage illustrations and ephemera are either by Marilyn Stablein or from the artist's collection.
The text of Houseboat on the Ganges & A Room in Kathmandu retains a few of the anglicized names for cities like Benares (Hindi, Varanasi) and Bombay (Hindi, Mumbai) since they were the most commonly used place names in books and tourist brochures as well as signs at railway stations and shops in the sixties.

Copyright 2019
By Marilyn Stablein

Published by:
Chin Music Press
1501 Pike Place #329
Seattle, WA 98101
www.chinmusicpress.com

First (1) edition
Cover art & photographs by Marilyn Stablein
Book design by Carla Girard

ISBN978-1-63405-972-5

Library of Congress Cataloging in Publication data is available.

"Every day is a journey, and the journey itself home."

Matsuo Basho
Narrow Road to the Deep North

In memory of my father Paul Zulch and especially my mother, Thelma H. Zulch, who encouraged me to follow my curiosity and then received, read, and saved my letters for seven years. With love and gratitude.

My studies here are indispensible. Keith has a tibetan teacher now so he is quite busy. If I were to send some material for a skirt address for Margaret — how long does she wear them now? (inches) Don what size shirt? Bill also? waist down

My newest tool is a Rapido graph — a fine pen used for drafting but also very useful in drawing and pen sketching. Love to All. Happy Anniversary

and eternal joy,

Love
Marilyn

BY AIRMAIL
PAR AVION
हवाई पत्र
AEROGRAMME

पहला मोड़   इस पत्र

FIRST FOLD

Kashi
Jan. 69

Dear Mom & Dad, & GANG
  Glad you received a package. The carpet
should arrive shortly. Yesterday was a
[g]reat festival dedicated to the Goddess
[Sar]asvati - goddess of the arts and especially
[mus]ic. It also was the beginning of the Spring
[seas]on. Many colorful tents and shop windows,
[and] patios turned into temples showing images of
[the] goddess riding on a swan and playing
[up]on, colorful lights and music and incense
[all] the city - everywhere she could be
[seen] and felt. [And today is bright and sunny,
[cer]tainly very spring-like] I think the
[...] was a great help. Firstly I've been very
[well] and enjoyed a winter free from even
[a cold] which is unusually perfect. My hair is
[very] healthy and more abundant (ironically
[...] - as it seems to become more lovely

the more I contemplate that I must be free
from this attachment - that is to shave my
hair and thus clear the air. But I also
know that one doesn't have to become a monk
or a nun to lead a spiritual and monastic-like
life. So also can I
regard my hair. All and Everything is in
the MIND. Sorry to hear you were sick (I
So if our thoughts are pure so will be our actions.
think another reason is. that I kept warm
with more clothing than I had last year (tights))
And very important to keep your head, neck and
feet warm, Mom. Please take care and stay well.
Unfortunately I received neither of the first two drafts -
can you get refund? and send to % Mandelbaum because
I did get the last one you sent. Thank you for
all the trouble & concern. I went to the dentist for
the first time in a long while - and am relieved that
it wasn't too difficult, painful or expensive! India
is really complete with everything you want, need
and of what you never expected. Where is Alice
working and what sort of job does she have? Received
a nice letter from Diana - she seems quite
happy at Berkeley and even planning to come
East - perhaps. My plans are not formed but

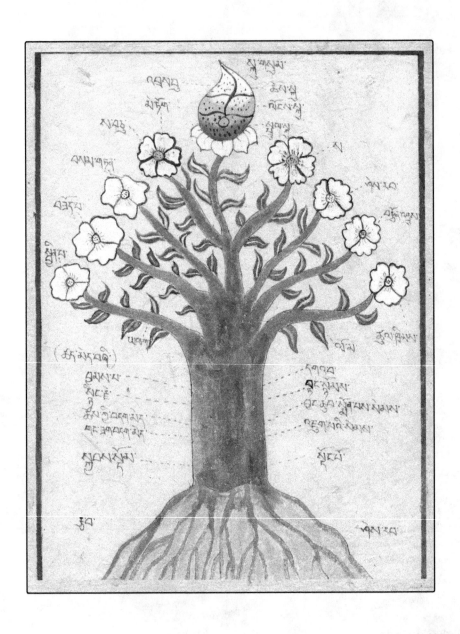

Houseboat on the Ganges
&
A Room in Kathmandu

Letters from India + Nepal
1966-1972

Visas

Visas

SEEN AT THE
ROYAL NEPALESE EMBASSY
WASHINGTON, D. C.
GOOD FOR ONE JOURNEY
TO NEPAL WITHIN SIX MONTHS
OF DATE HEREOF IF
PASSPORT REMAINS VALID.
THIS VISA SHALL BE VALID FOR
FIFTEEN DAYS AFTER ENTRY.
(SIGNED)
DATE   SEP 15 1967
NO.

FEE PAID $ 1.00

"TOURISM, PASSPORT TO PEACE"

7

Contents

A Note on the Letters

Half a century ago, before internet travel reservations, access to online listings and reviews of hotels, restaurants, train, bus, and ferry schedules; before online maps of historic sites and attractions; before internet banking, e-mail, cell phones, skype, scanners, and faxes, I left home at eighteen, my only belongings crammed into a dusty backpack, to hitchhike from Istanbul overland to India after a year of travels in North Africa, Europe, and England.

I was curious about Asia growing up in the far West between the foothills of the Santa Cruz mountains and the San Francisco Bay. On family trips to Half Moon Bay I loved watching the sun turn a tangerine gold before slowing sinking into the great exotic, pulsing, and restless Pacific Ocean. Staring out into the blue expanse and limitless sky my imagination swelled with a host of storybook and cinematic images gleaned from my growing awareness of the mysterious lands beyond the ocean. Later I'd learn how the Pacific Rim countries and states including California, Oregon and Washington, were connected in a vast global community spread out over twenty thousand miles of shared shoreline.

I felt at home in San Francisco's Chinatown where I shopped for inexpensive hand-painted paper fans and Chinese paper lanterns. I wandered the aisles of Cost Plus in Palo Alto and found Christmas presents for my family. Japan was the source of cheap and exotic toys and knick-knacks after the war. I noticed porcelain trinkets like salt shakers and ceramic dogs and cats stamped at the bottom: "Made in Occupied Japan." I wore *tabis,* those black cotton slippers with openings next to the big toes so my cloth-covered feet could easily slip into oriental thong sandals or summer flip-flops.

One Christmas my father gave me a book of Chinese fairy tales. I'd fall asleep envisioning jade princesses and the ghosts who haunted the dark footpaths through Chinese forests. Stone or metal Buddha statues, pagoda temples and palaces, reverberating temple gongs, Chinese junks and jade necklaces all sprang to life in crazy travel fantasies. More than once I daydreamed about the blue willow dishes we ate dinner on—the lovers separated by a circular foot-bridge like the one I awkwardly climbed up and over on school field trips to the Japanese Tea Garden in San Francisco's Golden Gate Park.

On game nights around the dining room table, father taught us to play Parcheesi, a game that originated in India—the name derives from the Sanskrit *panca*, five, and *vimsati*, twenty, referring to twenty-five, the highest throw. My favorite game was *World Traveler* with the unfolding game board map of the world's oceans and continents. Players traveled jump by jump to every exotic corner of the world. The first to circle the globe won.

When I visited a school chum of Japanese descent, a gold Buddha with heavy eyelids serenely graced a sideboard in the living room. At the entry to a Chinese friend's home, a figurine of the Goddess of Mercy Kwan Yin rose gracefully above a bowl of incense ash in an alcove by the front door.

I biked everywhere, thrilled with the freedom to explore neighborhoods on my own. One day as I bicycled down Middlefield Road in Palo Alto, I noticed a sign for a Buddhist temple. Curious, I parked my bike and went to investigate. A Japanese caretaker kindly showed me the Buddha statue on an altar decorated with flowers and plants. Later I asked my mother to drive me back for a spring Bonsai plant sale.

A Japanese Zen priest, Suzuki Roshi, helped popularize Buddhism and Zen meditation. Alan Watts, an English Zen Buddhist scholar, who lived on a houseboat in Sausalito, California first linked Zen with the Beats in his essay, "Beat Zen, Square Zen and Zen".[1] His *The Art of Zen* lectures, which regularly aired on Pacifica radio KPFA, sparked my interest as did the work of Paul Reps, one of the first American haiku poets to write about his travels and studies in China and Japan beginning in the 1940s. His books *Zen Telegrams* and *Zen Flesh, Zen*

1. Alan Watts, *Beat Zen, Square Zen, and Zen,* Chicago Review, 1958.

Bones, were bestselling mass market paperback titles.

Japanese programs frequently appeared on educational television. Every Tuesday evening, I reserved an hour (no small feat in a family of eight) to follow along with T. Mikami, a Japanese brush painting master, on his channel 9, KQED art show. He first introduced me to sumi ink brush paintings of Mt. Fuji, pine cones, lobsters, and fish.

I checked out books on haiku from the Palo Alto Public Library. The travels of the wandering ascetic *Siddhartha,* in the novel by Herman Hesse, brought early Buddhist history and philosophy to life in a world literature class in high school.

I first saw Satyajit Ray's *Apu Trilogy* at a Sunday night film series at Stanford University a mile from my home. If I were to name two influences that have informed my life, the first would be the love of art, the other an abiding interest in Asian and Southeast Asian culture and philosophy.

In the sixties I read Jack Kerouac's *On the Road* and took day trips to North Beach, home of a thriving poetry scene in San Francisco. Political unrest came to the U.C. campus my freshman year. Mario Savio, spokesman and strategist for Berkeley's fiery Free Speech Movement, personified the angry young men and women who weren't afraid to stand up against the establishment and support important causes like free speech, women's equality, and the right to vote.

The Peace Corps offered opportunities to volunteer in developing communities. Study Abroad Programs lured college students like me to leave home, study overseas, and reap the rewards of living and working in totally new environments in foreign countries.

In 1965 with a round trip charter flight ticket to Europe—I tore up the return ticket in Paris three months later—I arrived in London where I soon discovered Watkins Books, London's oldest occult bookshop, established in 1893, and read about the English Buddhist scholars Edward Conze and Christmas Humphries, the theosophist Annie Besant and British and European women explorers to the Middle East, India and Tibet like Alexandra David Neel, Freya Stark and Isabella Byrd, a 19th century explorer. I first tasted curries and biryanis at East Indian restaurants and browsed in East Indian markets.

I bought a silver dragon head ring embedded with turquoise and coral stones made in Nepal at the open-air Porto Bello market.

This was the poetic, social, cultural, and political milieu from which I emerged, a young woman in her teens, who made a life-changing decision in 1966 to travel overland to Asia the long, slow way, in the footsteps of beat poets Gary Snyder, Allen Ginsberg and Joanne Kyger who arrived by boat and plane to trek the same dusty pilgrimage trails four years ahead of me. Although their Indian travel logs and journals were not published until the 1970s and 1980s, I heard about them in India.[2]

When I rented a room in a Tibetan monastery in Dalhousie, India, a few of the young Tibetan monks at the Young Lamas' Home School remembered Allen Ginsberg's bushy beard and his visit to Dalhousie. Another time, Yogi Chen in his retreat in Kalimpong shared a handwritten letter from Gary Snyder, who described a parcel of back-country land he recently acquired outside of Nevada City, California. His plans for the land echoed my own yearning to someday settle down in a quiet country setting to grow herbs and vegetables, paint, and write—plans I shared in a few letters I wrote home from the road.

Enamored of the beat jazz poet pilgrim travelers who came before me, and the community of monks, spiritualists, wanderers, scholars, and artists I encountered along the way, I was moved to stay on in India after my three-month tourist visa expired. The letters I wrote home in *Houseboat on the Ganges & A Room in Kathmandu* begin in Athens and cover my arrival in Bombay and travels around India and Nepal.

After four years studying the spiritual traditions and art of India, Nepal and Tibet, my lifestyle changed dramatically when I married a Columbia University Tibetan and Sanskrit scholar, in a Newari ceremony in the Queen's forest outside of Kathmandu. We started our family in a walk-up apartment with running water and electricity—enviable and rare modern conveniences at the time—but there

---

2. Gary Snyder's *Passage Through India*, was first published in 1971; Allen Ginsberg's *Indian Journals*, in 1970 and Joanne Kyger's *Japan and India Journals* appeared in 1981.

was no kitchen, refrigerator, sink, or glass in the shuttered windows. I cooked on a single burner kerosene camping stove.

Houseboat on the Ganges & A Room in Kathmandu contains seven years of letters I wrote home describing life and travels on the back roads, unpaved Himalayan footpaths and ancient pilgrimage trails in the far east where I studied art, calligraphy, and Buddhism.

Marilyn

Our walk-up apartment in Kathmandu.

My Nepali kitchen–a hotplate on a straw mat.

ONE

Houseboat
on the
Ganges

Athens, Greece
August 31, 1966

Just left Crete, the Palace of Knossos, the Minoan civilization, the bare-breasted serpent-clutching Goddess behind and headed with Keith Dowman, my English boyfriend, back to the mainland. We really enjoyed Crete's warm, sunny days, blue Mediterranean seas, and beautiful skies. Sirocco winds from North Africa blew constantly through the village. Last year at this time I was in Egypt a short distance from Crete.

August is grape season on Crete. We took a short job picking grapes to make into raisins. How hard and hot the work is—twelve-hour days from 6 a.m. to 6 p.m. with only a 90-minute break for lunch. I hadn't worked so hard for a small wage since I pitted apricots for two weeks that summer alongside migrant workers in Mountain View. Pitting apricots and spreading them flat on a tray was tedious. The gypsies are hard workers. Too bad I got dysentery from eating so many of those delicious grapes!

In Athens the mail situation is next to impossible. Your last letter of July 21 took one month to arrive. Did you get my two letters from Crete? Since I'll be on the road for a while, I'll have to let you know a month in advance where I'll be. That way I can be sure letters will arrive. The drawback: I won't be getting mail as frequently.

Today Greece. Tomorrow Istanbul.

Istanbul, Turkey
September 10, 1966

We decided to head east. We'll be in Istanbul for two weeks—not long enough to receive mail. My next definite address will be c/o American Express, Hamilton House, Block A, Connaught Place, New Delhi, INDIA. I won't be there for over a month, but I look forward to hearing from you then.

I hope the Iranian earthquakes have subsided. We plan to go

through that area on our overland route to India. Both Hinduism and Buddhism originated in India. I can't think of a better place to study these spiritual traditions than in the country of their origin.

Fortunately, India and Pakistan are inexpensive. Otherwise I don't know how I'd manage moneywise. I'll look into the possibility of teaching English. I could tutor students or see about setting up a class at a university. On second thought, if the standard of living is low, I'm sure wages are low, too. Anyway, I'm not starving yet.

Karachi, Pakistan

October 1966

My apologies for not writing since Athens—have done a lot of hard traveling—mainly non-stop except for a few days rest in Tehran and western Pakistan—not by choice. The Iranian bus didn't cross the border into Pakistan and the only train going east didn't arrive for three days. We waited at a desert tea shop that sold bottled soft drinks—a luxury here. There is less chance of getting dysentery if we avoid well water and drink only bottled drinks. The owner fed us at night: rice, chickpea stew, eggplant, and slices of tomato marinated in lemon juice.

Karachi is very hot and sticky. We're the guests of the parents of an old school buddy of Keith's. They're attached to the British diplomatic service. Since we're not married, we have separate bedrooms in their large and rambling house—like an Eichler, or a ranch house back home.

If things go as planned, we'll catch a boat to Bombay in a few days. I plan to do some very easy, ascetic living: intensive reading and studying Hindu scriptures like the Upanishads, the Bhagavad Gita, and the Ramayana in the solitude of the Himalayas in Nepal. I'll begin with Hindu writings then branch out to Buddhist writings.

Ever since I attended a lecture in London at the Tibet Society I've been fascinated by Tibetan philosophy and mysticism. Travel to Tibet is impossible, however, since the Chinese invaded the country in 1959. Many Tibetan refugees live in Nepal and Northern India now so it's possible to study Tibetan and meet Tibetans outside of Tibet.

After Nepal, I want to go to Benares, to the sprawling Benares Hindu University, and see if it's possible to study Hindu philosophy in English. English used to be the national language of India before Independence twenty years ago. A lot has changed since then.

New Delhi, India
November 15, 1966

Just arrived in New Delhi yesterday during the Diwali festival of lights.To celebrate, people carry candles in street processions and pull carts with clay statues of the goddess Durga who has multiple arms and sits astride a tiger, a symbol of her strength and fearlessness.

Fireworks fill the night skies. Family members exchange gifts like we do at Christmas. My favorite scene: twisted cotton wicks burning in hundreds of little hand-made clay bowls filled with the oil of clarified butter or ghee. Lights rim every window sill and line the roofs of houses and temples. Soft, flickering lights everywhere.

We had a pleasant journey from Bombay. Since I'm very interested in Buddhism and Buddhist art, Keith and I visited the Buddhist cave temples at Ellora. Next, we saw the superb frescos at Ajanta. The beautifully detailed cave paintings date from the second century BC.

All of the wall paintings depict scenes of the Buddha's life: his mother's auspicious dream of conception when a white elephant entered her side before his birth; the Buddha's first steps; the young prince's disenchantment with palace life when he left home to try to understand the meaning of the suffering he saw outside the palace; his fast, meditation and enlightenment under the Bodhi tree, and finally the Buddha surrounded by disciples as he taught and lectured.

There is so much to see. We also stopped at Sanchi where three ancient stupas (pagoda-like monuments) were erected to house or memorialize some of the Buddha's relics. Originally his body was divided into seven parts. Each part was placed inside a stupa located in different parts of India.

There are no hotels near the ancient Buddhist pilgrimage sites. Conveniently most of the historical sites have guesthouses. We stayed in a dak bungalow, originally built to house British officials when they traveled on business from one district to another.

Agra is a good city for shopping. I bought a sari, the dress that the Indian women wear. A sari is five yards of cloth which women carefully wrap around their waists and torsos. It takes some practice to put it on right—no buttons, zippers or snaps to help keep the cloth in place. It also takes practice to walk in one or climb stairs without tripping on the front pleats.

The Taj Mahal is really a magnificent structure, a romantic tribute to the Mughal emperor Shah Jahan's beloved wife Mumtaz Mahal who died in childbirth. The walls are marble inlaid with ornate semi-precious stones like coral, jade, and lapis.

Tomorrow we'll visit the Ladakh Buddhist Vihara, a temple, library and living quarters on the banks of the Jumna river in New Delhi built by Tibetan refugees. The library is very complete, with an extensive collection of books written in English on Tibet, as well as translations, and ancient Tibetan palm-leaf manuscripts.

Even though it is the festive Diwali season for the Hindus in Delhi, in other parts of India people are really starving. The monsoons failed to bring enough water to grow a decent crop of wheat. The already existing perennial shortage of grain is now in even shorter supply. Food is cheap, but the people are so poor they cannot afford to buy adequate amounts to feed their children. There are also many diseases like cholera, malaria, leprosy, and typhoid.

But don't worry about me. Luckily, I have been in perfect health. My interior is hardened, and I seem to resist minor infections. I even drink the local water with no trouble.

I want to study or devote time to meditation at a Buddhist monastery, but I haven't located one yet. Benares is a center of Buddhist thought and pilgrimage.Send mail to me next c/o Central Post Office, Benares, Uttar Pradesh, INDIA.

Kathmandu, Nepal
December 20, 1966

It's very cold here but blue skies and warm, sunny afternoons take
the chill off. Kathmandu valley is 5000 feet above sea level, nestled
between snowcapped Himalayas. The valley is fertile. Two rivers
meander across the narrow plain.

Yesterday we walked three miles west of Kathmandu to a Buddhist
monastery on a hill overlooking the valley. The hill is inhabited by
hundreds of monkeys. The monks at Swayambhunath were busy
preparing puja (a ritual) for the rice harvest festival held the twenty-first day of December, the first day of winter. Rice is first offered to
the gods and later everyone partakes of the rice cakes.

Kathmandu has a unique population which includes Tibetan
Buddhists, Nepalese Hindus, tribal villagers, Gurkha warriors with
khukuri knives, Sherpas, Newars Buddhists, mountain villagers,
Chinese, and foreigners from Europe and America. The restaurants
serve mostly Tibetan and Chinese dishes. The city has an abundance
of shrines, intricately carved temples, and very old stupas. The eyes
painted on the exterior of the large stupas ward off evil and represent
the "third eye," which is a mystical symbol for extra sensory perception and clairvoyance.

The tantric practices of the Buddhists are very difficult to
decipher. I hope to gain some sort of understanding, some compre-
hension that unites the physical and the spiritual.

Burmese Pilgrim's Rest House
Sarnath, India
January 18, 1967

I now have a semi-permanent address for the winter—at least
through March. Sarnath is a holy city for Buddhists. The Buddha
delivered his first sermon, "The Turning of the Wheel of Dharma"
at the Deer Park here. He set the wheel in motion, so to speak,

Stupa with view of Kathmandu valley.

explaining his theory of the Wheel of Life—a theory of reincarnation. The village is very small, located ten miles from Benares. The Chinese, Tibetans, Ceylonese (or Sinhalese), Burmese and the Maha Bodhi Society all have monasteries in town.

The Deer Park is extensive. Benches are set between the flower beds and the wide, open lawns. A unique way to cut the grass here— harness a cow to pull a mower. A fenced in area protects a dozen or so small deer which have been reintroduced into the enclosure. The remains of one of the largest stupas dominates the landscape.

We have a room at the Burmese Rest House, or *vihara,* outside the western gate to the park. To get to the village to shop I walk through the park grounds.

On weekdays I hire a horse and carriage and ride into Benares to the university where I am enrolled as a "casual student" to attend lectures and use the library. The department of Indology incorporates Indian philosophy, art and history. There are quite a few foreign (English speaking) students who attend the university. Some are on a Junior Year Abroad program. The most interesting classes are those for graduate students.

At Sarnath we do our own cooking over hot charcoal every night. We drink buffalo milk, eat meat rarely (twice a week) and live mostly on duck eggs, rice, potatoes, and vegetables like cabbage, carrots, and eggplant. There are a limited number of vegetables available in the street stalls. Since the atmosphere at Sarnath is conducive to quiet meditative self-study, I have been reading and thinking a lot.

Sarnath, India
February 25, 1967

The tenth marks the height of spring festivities. Benares is the abode of Shiva, the Hindu god of Creation as well as Destruction. On the new moon in March pilgrims from all over India come to Benares to bathe in the sacred, purifying waters of the Ganges. Following tributes to Shiva, the Hindus celebrate a festival characterized by a wild exchange of colors.

Everyone participates in *Holi*. Friends and strangers throw colors at each other. No one is spared a wild color bath. People wear old clothes. The rowdiest revelers use spray guns and gooey, thick paint. Most people toss colored powders like dry poster paint without the water added.

At five p.m. the color throwing suddenly subsides. Crowds walk to the banks of the river to bathe and change into brand new white clothing. Dressed in their spotless white flowing saris, kurtas, and pajamas, the people visit the temples and act as if nothing unusual happened earlier.

The hot season is approaching and with it comes an abundance of flies, mosquitos, malaria, and other diseases. It's time to head north again. This time we'll visit the Indian Himalayas in Kashmir until the monsoons subside.

The elections have stirred up a lot of trouble, especially in the villages. India is in dire need of a sound government; the future looks grim.

I enjoy painting temple motifs I copy from the Tibetan monastery: symbolic arrangements of incense, flowers, fruits, and musical instruments.

To sketch the figure of the Buddha I need to construct an elaborate linear grid. There is no guesswork or free-form Buddha images; every measurement is precise. The head, shoulders, arms, and feet must conform to a certain set of proportions.

The spices are excellent. Anything can be made edible. I'm adept at cooking curries, pilaus, and unleavened bread, or chapati. My chapati, however, is never as round as the ones the Indian women make by slapping dough between their palms—they don't even use rolling pins!

If I boil buffalo milk, add a tablespoon of yoghurt as a starter, pour the mixture into a large clay bowl and let it stand overnight, in the morning I have fresh yoghurt.

We left Sarnath and moved to Benares to live in a houseboat on the river. The *ghats,* the riverside steps, are the busiest areas of the city. Everyone, young, old, poor or rich, crowds onto the huge cement steps to dunk in the waters of the Ganges. It's fascinating to observe all walks of life from my one-room houseboat docked at Dashashwamedh, the busiest *ghat*.

A houseboat on the Ganges.

Varanasi, India

March 9, 1967

Today is one of the holiest days in India. The celebrations are
especially enthusiastic in Benares, home of Shiva, since tonight is
Shivaratri or Shiva's night.

Our houseboat, a single open room, is docked at the end of the
main *ghat.* Hundreds of Hindu pilgrims walk down the steps daily
to bathe. They choose this particular spot (our front yard!) to free
themselves from their sins since this is where Shiva purged himself.
The Ganges worshippers are fanatical: scores and scores of men,
women and children all day long make the journey up and down the
huge cement steps. Temples line the river; bells clang continuously.
The noise never stops. Tonight, I expect the festivities will reach a
climax.

Yesterday we met an ex-surfer from Malibu, a tall long-haired
blond guy who wanders around India dressed as a sadhu. He was
bathing in the river, eyes closed deep in meditation when I first
spotted him, the only fair-skinned bather in a mass of fanatical Ganga
worshippers. I invited him in for tea which he readily accepted. We
reminisced about home and the pleasures we missed: jazz, coffee
shops in North beach, foods like avocados and artichokes. His
Hindu name is Bhagavan Das.

Did you receive the presents I sent? The Tibetan prayer book and
prayer beads are for Sully. The embroidered yellow cashmere cape
is for Alice. May everyone enjoy the human thigh bone trumpet
from Tibet and the printed prayers on rice paper. My confidence in
the Indian mail system is quite low so let me know if and when the
package arrives. The mail, like the trains, functions but nothing is
guaranteed.

My future is quite bright here. I don't feel the rush to return home
and re-enroll at Berkeley for my sophomore year. My freshman year
was amazing with the birth of the Free Speech Movement but many
of my classes were cancelled. Are students still staging protests?

I learn more by just living here and traveling than I did in a crowded Berkeley classroom watching a professor's lecture via short circuit television. Here I study, draw and paint. My twenty-first birthday is still a way off.

My wish for you: peace and happiness, both temporal and spiritual, in this life and the next.

Varanasi, India

March 28, 1967

This postcard features the famous lion column which is now the emblem of India. Lions stare out from the four directions. The original is located in Sarnath where it was erected 2,000 years ago. Today we leave for Delhi, the first step in our monsoon move up into the hills. The British seasonally moved up to the Himalayas, even moving their capital from Delhi in the winter to Simla during the monsoon summers.

Spring has come to this city. The women wear beautiful yellow, pink, and turquoise saris.

New Delhi, India

April 4, 1967

On the trip to Delhi we stopped at Lucknow then took a bus to visit an Indian friend, Harish Johari, who lives with his family in Bareilly. He taught us an ancient Hindu game called Leela which was the inspiration, no doubt, for our family board game, Snakes and Ladders. Players roll the dice and amble uphill through seventy-two squares with names like: plane of karma, atonement, clarity of consciousness. The goal is to reach the top, pass the "plane of bliss" and other ethereal sounding realms to arrive at "the phenomenal world."

If a player lands on a square with feathers of an arrow, he or she is thrust or jumps higher up the meandering path on the game board. If one lands on a snake head, on the other hand, he or she is swallowed and carried downhill sometimes fifty or sixty squares. The Indian game is played out like a spiritual quest.

Remember how we played Parcheesi around the dining room table? Parcheesi also originated in India.

I had a bad case of dysentery in Benares. The doctor recommended some pills for vitamin deficiency and a special diet which I've been following. Diet is especially important in India, essential to my general well-being. My vegetarian diet consists of eggs, rice, fresh vegetables, fruits, and unleavened bread.Sometimes I cook fresh fish. For an extra treat we'll eat cashew nuts mixed with honey. My aim is to strive for a natural diet. Gandhi claimed man's natural diet consists of the fruits and herbs which naturally grow in abundance. By nature, man is not a carnivorous animal. Of course, the Hindus strongly believe in the benefits of a vegetarian diet. Cooks pay careful attention to harvesting and preparing food. The best food in India is vegetarian.

The hot season is about to descend on the plains. In the mountains there are quite a few ashrams that offer instruction in yoga and meditation. Almora, a holy city, is considered a gateway to the Himalayas—source of the greatest rivers, a real land of the gods. Pilgrims in earlier times made the pilgrimage from Almora on foot over the Himalayas into Tibet.

We hope to stay in an ashram in Almora during the summer. By minimizing physical activity and finding a suitable place to continue my studies, I hope to continue my spiritual practice and read more. I shopped in Delhi bookstores to find books to read and last me throughout the monsoon. There are no English bookstores where I'm headed.

Did I tell you about the exquisite Persian miniature paintings? They are wonderfully detailed, full of color and precision. I'd like to copy some of the motifs. India is still a source of so much knowledge, history, and art not to forget the sensual pleasures of food, music, and dance. My enthusiasm never wanes.

Write to me c/o Central Post Office, Poste Restante, Almora, Uttar Pradesh, INDIA.

Almora
Uttar Pradesh
May 20, 1967

I'm adapting to mountain life quite well. Aside from a water shortage which means I must hire a boy to carry buckets up the mountain to the cottage, cooking is quite manageable. Since there isn't any form of transportation—not even horses for hire—I've grown accustomed to walking the two miles from our bungalow into town. We make the trip twice a week.

The other day I walked with Keith six miles to visit Lama Anagarika Govinda, a German scholar and Tibet traveler. I just finished his book, *Foundations of Tibetan Mysticism*. He has a brilliant mind and the verbal skills to lucidly express himself. One of his theories is that if philosophical concepts are produced diagrammatically or in a geometric context, they stand a good chance of being true, or universal.

This is also an important concept for me. In my art work I strive to incorporate both the intellectual and the visual, or physical. I promised to send him a sample of one of my diagrams. I traced the numbers of a magic square engraved in brass on the door of the Niranjani akhara temple courtyard where we lived in Benares. I translated the numbers into English then I connected the squares in a numerical order and produced a star-like diagram, similar to one of Lama Govinda's diagrams. Albrecht Durer the 16th century master German printmaker and artist also experimented with magic squares of numbers. Whichever way you add the numbers in rows, that is, up, down, across or diagonally, the sum of each row is always the same.

Lama Govinda has a profound knowledge of the Tantras. Perhaps you're familiar with Timothy Leary's *Psychedelic Experience* or Evans Wentz's *Tibetan Book of the Dead*?

Lama Govinda wrote forewords to both although they are not necessarily profound works. Li Gotami, Lama Govinda's wife and an accomplished artist, served us tall glasses of Kool-Aid which really quenched our thirst after the long walk. It reminded me of the pitchers of lime Kool-Aid we made to cool off in those hot Palo Alto summers. I saw Li Gotami's watercolors of her Tibet travels at the museum in Bombay when we first arrived in India.

An interesting coincidence is that Leary wrote his book of poems, *Psychedelic Prayers,* when he lived in the cottage where we now live. It is a peaceful home and a good place to write and read although last week, I was baffled by loud thumps followed by noisy footsteps across the tin roof. We went outdoors to investigate. Nothing. The next afternoon the same thump followed by scampering. This time we noticed a small animal leap off a tall pine tree and coast or float down to our roof. My first sighting of a flying squirrel! Or, more accurately a gliding squirrel.

The atmosphere in Almora is certainly conducive to meditation: the peace and solitude of the forests, the surrounding snow-capped Himalayas, the river Kosi far below winding a path through the valley. Consequently, I've been doing a lot of reading and quiet study which is the only way to begin to understand mysticism, yoga, the tantras, and meditation.

An interesting Danish man, Sunyabhai, who's in his seventies, lives in a cave-like dwelling on Crank's Ridge—a nickname for the ridge where a number of foreigners like Lama Govinda and his wife live. I covet his incredible library. Books in English are difficult to find.

My address will be Poste Restante, Almora, until the rains hit in about a month and a half.

Almora

Uttar Pradesh

June 1, 1967

Travel is exhilarating. So many new experiences and so many things to see, interpret and respond to. I'm glad that Alice is touring Europe. Now that another daughter is enraptured with travel you might better understand why I've postponed my return to continue my own travels.

If anyone plans to travel this far east he or she needs to adjust to cold showers. It's really not that bad. The water is cool, not frigid. I heat a pot of hot water and splash myself with a cup dipped into a warm bucket of water in frigid weather.

Every traveler has unique experiences. My ideal way to travel is to lessen as much as possible the barriers that separate me from the local people. I strive to integrate as much as possible. In other words, I gladly sacrifice comforts and customs in order to learn another way of life. Person to person, culture to culture—I learn by living. I don't plan to starve, die from thirst or suffer like many unfortunate villagers. But I do wear India dress, eat Indian food, speak Tibetan and Hindi (a little), and generally accept local customs like not eating meat or drinking alcohol.

The water shortage is acute. A few natural springs have dried up for the first time since this area has been inhabited. The monsoons will alleviate the rising temperatures. Hopefully only five more weeks until the deluge, although the precise arrival time is always a matter of speculation.

I read that sun spots and surface explosions on the sun's perimeter affect, not only the weather on earth, but man's psychic centers as well. The waves of vibrations interfere with man's polar magnetism. Some scientists claim mental insanity, retardation, and other derangements are indirectly caused by the sun's vibrations. Anyway, that's one theory in a universe of many theories. Life evolves; life endures; eventually all life terminates.

Almora

Uttar Pradesh

June 25, 1967

Enclosing a photo, we recently had taken in Almora. Keith is wearing a saffron colored cloth and Hindu prayer beads. I'm in a bright red sari.

We've been living and traveling together for two years already, since

Crete—and before that, we wintered in London. It was my idea to visit India. After studying a term at Benares Hindu University, he is convinced that the real mastery of eastern wisdom must come from within. Any wisdom is but wisdom of oneself.

Keith has a sociology background from the London School of Economics but is deeply interested, as I am, in studying Buddhism, meditation, the Indian way of life and the rich heritage of ancient India.

A guru might be helpful but to be one's own guru is better. When I master some of the elementary essentials of meditation and philosophical thought, then I'll feel ready to move on, carrying the wisdom within.

When I am confident that India has been experienced as fully as practical, I will return to the west. I'm tentatively in the process of returning—albeit slowly. Keith's brother lives in Australia and we thought about returning via the Pacific to complete the circle (or cycle) which for me began in California. Air and boat fares over the Pacific, however, are expensive.

I'm anxious to return home and reconnect with family and friends. The longer I'm away the more the memories seem to fade. A memory may conjure up experiences, but experiences can never be relived. Change is the basis of life; the wheel of life revolves. Life continues as a timeless, constant stream of events and non-events. Only the essence, the soul/spirit, is absolute and unchangeable.

But I'm not ready to return yet. I'll let you know when that time comes.

Last week we trekked thirty miles to a nearby peak, Mirtola. It was a beautiful walk: up ridges, down the other side, up again. The Himalayas, the views, the air, the immensity is so inspiring. This week I'm exhausted.

Dharamsala

Himachal Pradesh

August 8, 1967

We're touring the Kangra Valley, located in the Himalayas near Almora. We visited His Holiness the Dalai Lama who settled here after his flight from Tibet. He is a warm, spiritual man. His sincerity and happiness radiate and inspire all who meet him. He is truly one of the saintly.

    —Oops—the bus to Pathankot leaves in 5 minutes. Gotta run.

    (Later...) We're traveling to Kashmir which lies between Pakistan, Russia, and Chinese occupied Tibet. I'll write more when I arrive and get settled.

Srinagar

Kashmir

August 23, 1967

The month of August seems particularly fortuitous. Last week, with the encouragement of Ram Dass, Keith and I made a pilgrimage to the Amarnath cave located in a glacial area of northern Kashmir, near the border with Tibet. The ancient holy cave is an abode of Shiva. What's so unique about this particular cave, is the enormous *lingam* (phallus statue) naturally formed out of ice. The ice phallus rises and falls as the moon waxes and wanes. That is, on the full moon the ice sculpture reaches a height of six feet. The entire pilgrimage is sixty miles. The highest point on the journey is 15,000 feet. Utterly fantastic to see the glacial origins of the large rivers, the primeval snowy beauty and wilderness, nature totally uninhabited by man.

    On the way up to the cave we met a number of Hindu holy men. One, Neem Karoli Baba, was very playful and full of laughter. He always offered us food when we met him on the trail. Every time he saw us, he told his attendants to give us something to eat. We loved the apples, oranges, and bananas Baba literally showered on us by tossing the fruit from across the tent.

He laughed like a little boy as he watched us catch and eat the fruit. Food from a guru is said to be blessed. As we sat in our tent for the night at an altitude of 12,000 feet, we ate delicious milk sweets made and hand-carried by his devout pilgrims.

Luckily, we made friends with the Muslim outfitters who allowed us to sleep in canvas tents they pitched at rest stops along the trail to the cave. Kashmir is predominately, historically Muslim. The outfitters only asked a nominal charge from us but set exorbitant prices for the Hindu pilgrims who gladly paid the inflated "high pilgrimage season" rate. Every devout Hindu yearns to complete the Amarnath Yatra, a circuit of holy places that surrounds Shiva's ice cave.

We rented a houseboat on Dal Lake in Srinagar. The houseboats, originally built for vacationing Brits, are plush and nothing like our spartan, single room, Benares houseboat. This one has two bedrooms, a sofa, dining room table, chairs, and even a grand piano! Since many houseboats were empty we were able to bargain for an affordable "student low season" rate. A boat ride to Shalimar, a Mughal-inspired garden paradise on the other side of the lake, was idyllic. Hundreds of roses, lilies, carnations, and asters bloomed alongside floral walkways and garden pavilions. Turquoise kingfisher birds and hummingbirds drank from fountains and ponds.

Yesterday, my twenty-first birthday, passed quietly. I lost my youthful anxiety which used to accompany birthdays. I no longer think about what I want, what I crave. To me the passing of time is sobering. I'm more aware of the impermanence of this life. I concentrate more than I used to on the reality of the present.

Did I mention our audience with His Holiness the Dalai Lama, the spiritual head of the Tibetans? When we were in Dharamsala we met Richard Alpert, the former Harvard professor. He invited us to join him for an audience with His Holiness. He made the appointment since he wanted to interview him. His questions focused on the nature of altered states of consciousness. I was content receiving His Holiness' *darshan*, the Hindu custom of not talking but just sitting in the presence of a spiritual teacher.

Sometimes it's easier for me to communicate on a non-verbal level which is why I like the Hindu concept of *darshan*, or spiritual audience. It was enough just to sit and be present.

Alpert is a gifted storyteller. His tales of the changes and marvels in California were amazing. I've been away two years now. I'm anxious to return when I complete my studies. Reading the ancient scriptures like the Vedas gives me confidence and deep pleasure. Vedic philosophy, which originated in this cradle of civilization, is still alive in all parts of society.

New Delhi

August 31, 1967

On the return journey from Kashmir the bus driver asked passengers if they wanted to take a short side trip to stop at a famous water shrine located ten miles off the main road. The passengers whole-heartedly agreed. Since we didn't speak Kashmiri we didn't really have a vote in the matter, but we went along with the group. We walked around another beautiful Mughal garden and saw our reflections in the large pool, said to be the source of the Jumna river. There was no bathing. Large fish swam in the pool.

Later we stopped in Amritsar, a holy city for the Sikhs, a religious group distinguished by turbaned men and sword-carrying holy mendicants. Sikh men never cut their hair. They honor a very strong warrior tradition. They're fighters hoping to create a separate province or country adjacent to the predominantly Hindu India, sometimes called Hindustan. Painted frescos cover the interior of the Sikhs' Golden Temple built on an island in the center of an enormous architectural pool.

The outside walks are inlaid with marble in intricate maze-like patterns. This is one pattern I copied in my notebook. We joined other pilgrims for large communal meals of rice, dal, chapati, cauliflower, peas, potato and cabbage curries served by devout Sikh volunteers. At night we slept in the pilgrim hostel, or *dharamsala*.

I'll write next from Agra. We're heading south to visit Vrindavan where Lord Krishna was born.

New Delhi
September 15, 1967

During our stay in Vrindaban, Lord Krishna's birthplace, we visited a number of saints and holy people who reside in temples on the banks of the river Jumna. One swami in particular, Swami A.C. Bhaktivedanta, became our unofficial guru while we were there. At least he proclaimed as much. Perhaps you have heard of him? He was in San Francisco some months back initiating "Krishna Consciousness," his self-styled religious practice which aims to liberate mankind. By absorbing the idea of Krishna and chanting the maha mantra "Hari Krishna..." the Swami believes a practitioner can expand consciousness. Evidently, he and his devotees chanted in Golden Gate Park.

He is a very powerful personality and could easily inspire a creative response from those seeking a religious practice. He professes a disciplined escapism while adhering to the Hindu code of *brahmacharya*, a celibate practitioner. We disagreed, however, on one basic point: namely, why Krishna offered the *only* means to a universal higher consciousness? There are hundreds of other spiritual and religious figures to consider.

The Bhagavad Gita, a Hindu classic which depicts Krishna's life story, is a powerful and profound scripture but the Swami's narrow-mindedness prohibits him from accepting any other spiritual discipline as a means to a universal enlightenment or salvation. He invited us to set up an ashram for him in London. We politely declined. His personality, in fact, was overbearing and we were glad to leave.

Niranjani Akhara
Shivala Ghat Varanasi November 28, 1967

We just returned from a two-week visit to Bodh Gaya where Siddhartha Gautama, the Buddha, attained enlightenment after meditating one night under a peepal tree. The tree still stands, or at least an offshoot of the original tree. In addition, the temple has an impressive number of stone carvings and stupas from the early Buddhist days, although when the moguls swept across the plains of India, they desecrated many of the statues by lopping off noses, severing heads and arms.

We traveled with Tarthang Tulku and his Egyptian-born wife, Nazli. Tarthang teaches a Vajrayanist philosophy. We spent many hours meditating under his direction. I've always been attracted to the Buddhist teachings of mindfulness: purity of body, speech and mind; right action and supreme compassion for all human beings and all living organisms.

The mind throws up many roadblocks that interfere with thoughts and cause confusion. Meditation is like pulling the reins on a horse. I have to pull much harder in order to leash the desires that always arise in the mind. But even before I attempt to curb desires, I need to recognize what they are. Hence, mindfulness. Anyway, this might give you an idea of my practice.

Benares was complete chaos today. The Hindu student population of some several thousand rioted! All day. They protested the use of English as the official language. English is still used in the judicial system and in schools. Many newspapers and signs are still printed in English, a throwback to the era of the British raj when the British ruled India for a hundred years.

As students paraded up the *chowk,* or main market street, they ripped down every visible sign in English in the bazaar. They plastered paint over signposts, shouted, broke windows...and there I was shopping! Fortunately, the students did not make the connection between the English on the signs and the English-speaker shopping on the street. At any rate, I didn't hesitate to pull my shawl over my head—my instant disguise when in a dangerous situation. The police did nothing to stop the rampage. Once or twice the police reportedly opened fire but that didn't stop the angry mob.

To experience a crowd scene when panic suddenly breaks out and hundreds of Indians stampede, is really terrorizing. Fear is such a primitive and powerful feeling. Emotions and feelings may be "illusory" for Buddhists, but the spontaneously arising violent destruction and angry mob scenes were quite real to me! I will stop writing now as it is late and my sentences (as well as my senses) are jumbled.

Varanasi

February 9, 1968

A special treat last week was attending the annual music festival. Over four evenings musicians played classical *ragas* with sitar, tabla, veena, and sarod. The stage was set-up in a large colorful tent. Each evening the concert began at 8:00 p.m. and lasted throughout the night. Musicians played the last raga at 6:00 a.m. just as the sun rose dramatically over the serene, immense Ganges.

The first signs of spring: sunny blue skies and turquoise-tailed kingfishers I first noticed in Kashmir snagging fish from the river. Every morning we bathe in the Ganges. The river is believed to have the miraculous power to heal, cleanse, and revitalize the spirit. A daily bath is like a ritual incorporating worship, prayer, baptism, and blessings.

To get to the river I simply enter the Niranjani Akhara temple compound (to which our room is attached), cross a courtyard filled with shrines and banyan trees and walk down ancient stone steps. A gigantic wooden door opens onto a private bathing *ghat*. I feel like I'm walking through a medieval fortress. The key to unlock the twelve-foot high, four-inch thick wooden door is eight inches long!

Faith is an important factor in any action. Faith in oneself and faith in a supreme self which is also expressed through oneself. I am increasingly more receptive to Buddha and his teachings, especially the Mahayana and Vajrayana interpretation of the Tibetans. My receptivity does not represent a conversion from Christianity to Buddhism. Rather I feel an expanded awareness that helps me understand both philosophies. Essentially: love is everything. Compassion is universal.

P.S. Indian women do not wear underwear, at least to my knowledge. Consequently, there is none available in the bazaar. I am desperate for underwear...if you could please send me two pairs of bikini nylon briefs (black) and one bra (32 A) I'd be forever grateful!

Varanasi,

Uttar Pradesh

March 8, 1968

Thank you so much for taking the trouble with the package. I'm sorry to say, it never turned up! What a nuisance!

To escape the on-coming heat, we will move again to the Himalayas and continue Tibetan studies there. I've mastered the Tibetan *dbu chen* script and can write the letters, but I still have trouble reading and understanding the texts. Our Tibetan teacher, Tarthang Tulku, arranged for a lama to teach us for a few months in Simla. Poetry and *thangka* painting are the subjects I'm interested in.

The eastern system of instruction is a good one. The teacher-student relationship is of primary importance. Books are only used to clarify what the teacher has personally demonstrated, not by lectures, but by transferring knowledge on a personal basis. Peace is attained when one understands there is no "self." No "self" to identify with; no "self" to feel unhappy, no "self" to crave and fear...it is difficult to explain.

Many westerners misinterpret the traditional Hindu guru-disciple relationship. Maharishi Maheshi Yogi has many followers including the Beatles, but his motives seem blatantly commercial and relatively naive. Just now in Benares there is a film production crew from Hollywood filming a movie called "The Guru" with Rita Tushingham. If you get a chance to see it, I have a bit-part sitting on the deck of a houseboat singing with a group of rugged but happy rucksack travelers. The camera focus on us, then to the Rita character who turns to her boyfriend and says, "Isn't that the carefree life..." or something to that effect.

The extras are paid fifty rupees a day and treated to dinner at the tourist hotel. At first the American style roast potatoes and pot-roast seemed like a treat, but since I've been on a vegetarian diet the meat was hard to digest. As you can probably guess, the film does not capture the real spirit of eastern mysticism. The rupees came in handy, though, to purchase a much-needed *Tibetan Dictionary* which was reprinted recently.

The Ganges has a species of fresh water dolphin. As the weather gets warmer, I frequently spot them jumping above water, breathing and playing. Really a remarkable fish for a river! Sometimes a dolphin reaches a length of ten feet. I sit for many hours on the balcony of the Shiva temple and watch the water buffalos and dolphins amuse themselves in the river.

Varanasi

March 1968

I haven't written for some time because I've been away in Bodh Gaya. Bihar state is extremely hot and dry. There are seasonal famines and water shortages. I was so delighted to return to Benares and jump in the Ganges two or three times a day. The river is just minutes from my room, across a temple courtyard and down some steps. But by the time I climb back up the steps again, I'm already hot. The heat will stay now and grow more intense until it is so overpowering it's necessary to stay indoors in the shade.

I'm enclosing two pictures taken in Bodh Gaya. The mountain behind me has a cave where Buddha meditated. A Tibetan monastery is situated halfway up. I stayed in the cave for a short while. I brought my own dried foodstuffs, watched the stars and satellites glistening in a black night sky, and listened to the whooshes and squeaks of bats. Village lights twinkled below me.

We stayed at a Burmese Pilgrim *vihara* which, like the one in Sarnath, was built to accommodate Burmese Buddhists who travel to India on pilgrimage to visit the cities where the Buddha lived and taught. Buddhist pilgrims from Sri Lanka and Japan also travel to Bodh Gaya to pay their respects to the temple and to an offshoot of the original Bodhi tree. Scriptures reveal that Buddha sat under the tree for days until he gained enlightenment. Tibetans also believe Bodh Gaya is the spiritual and mythical axis or center of their cosmos.

We were the first westerners to stay at the guesthouse at the invitation of Sumangala, the resident abbot. He told me about a local teacher, Munindra-ji, who studied *Vipassana* meditation in Burma. I was happy when he agreed to visit the Burmese *vihara* and personally teach me. Within a short while a few Americans, Joseph Goldstein[3], was one, arrived and also began the study of the *Vipassana* form of meditation.

This year I spent the Holi festival in the village with my friend Maria Monroe from Vancouver, Washington. The women gathered together and covered each other in red, green, and blue powdered colors. You should have seen my hair! Some villagers wore new white cotton clothes to receive the colors. At times during the year on the street or in the market I saw a few men stand out from the crowd because their white cotton clothing was splotched with a riot of bright colors. Now I know why.

---

3. Joseph co-founded in 1975 an international Vipassana center, the Insight Meditation Society, in Barre, MA.

Manali

Himachal Pradesh

May 23, 1968

Manali, nestled between snow ranges on three sides, is located at the
Northern most tip of the Kullu Valley. The snowline is only six miles
away. This is a welcomed change from the intense heat in Benares.
We will stay here at least six weeks until the monsoons begin. Manali
has a large Tibetan population. Many traders strap their goods onto
the backs of ponies and pack mules to travel over the snows. They
sell rice, grains, flours, and dried fruits in Tibet.

When the Rohtang Pass is cleared of snow, we'll trek over the
13,000 foot pass into Lahaul, a district culturally closer to Tibet than
India. Lahaul is a Buddhist area and the Lahaulis have a distinct
dress, dialect, and customs. They are very friendly, too.

We share a two-story house with Steve Landsburg, a friend from
Benares who practices the surbahar, an Indian stringed instrument,
six to seven hours a day.

—You ask me when I am coming home. I wish I could set a
definite time. We decided to stay longer in India, I'm sorry to say. The
deeper we go into the study of the Tibetan way of life, the more we
realize the rewards will be greater if we study harder. What I mean to
say is: I want more time and experience living with and learning from
the people whose religion is so alive and all-encompassing. Not only
the Tibetans' language, but their dress, ornaments, music, and art
reflect their strong beliefs.

To make Tibetan tea each morning I boil a handful of tea leaves
broken off a coarse brick-like hunk of dried pressed tea from China.
Add salt, milk, and yak butter if available—the fermented butter
tastes like blue cheese. Churn the mixture in a large wooden tea
churn that looks like a butter churn. For lunch we eat *thukpa*, a soup
of noodles, meat, broth, and vegetables. This is a typical hearty
mountain diet. Since the mangos ripen during the monsoon season,
the kitchen corner of my cottage is never without a bowl full of those
luscious fruits. And lychees, too! Delicious!

The eastern traditions focus on knowledge of self. Teachings are realized with the mind, but the body is also important as a vehicle to understanding. The depth of internal experience, or meditation, is quite different from western philosophical practices. Since the feasibility of a return to the west and then another trip back to India is unrealistic, I want to make the most of my stay here now. Learning the Tibetan language will be a strong foundation to further any studies back home. Each experience is alive. Another year will show great advancement. There is plenty of time to finish my university studies later.

The Indian tradition divides life into four stages: childhood, student, householder and ascetic recluse or retiree. Now I'm in the student stage. My years of austere living, estranged from relations and removed from material influences and possessions is only a temporary stage in this tradition.

In September Keith will attend the Sanskrit University in Benares and take first year Tibetan. I will continue to study the arts and literature of Tibet. Although India is a country of extreme contrasts, it is a spiritual haven for holy people, places of worship, sacred thoughts and prayers.

Almora

Himachal Pradesh

Summer 1968

Our landlord in Almora is an English missionary, Mary Opligher, who volunteers at a village clinic she founded to help local villagers get basic over-the-counter medicines. She introduced me to the work of the Russian artist, Nicholas Roerich, who was nominated for a Nobel Peace Prize in 1929, forty years ago. One of his paintings hanging in her living room depicts a mystical Himalayan landscape, very evocative and dream-like.

His son, Svetoslav Roerich, lives in the lower Kullu Valley with his wife. I wrote in advance to inquire about visiting—a quick phone call isn't an option in these isolated regions. We took a bus to Naggar village and walked a mile to his home.[4] He also paints. The two-story wooden home is filled with portraits, landscapes and Himalayan scenes. We had an interesting visit. The garden setting was serene and conducive to the creative life of a foreign resident in the high mountains. His older brother George Roerich was a noted Tibetologist.

Rishikesh
July 1968

We arrived in Rishikesh to visit some friends in an ashram and perhaps meet Maharishi Maheshi Yogi, spiritual advisor to the Beatles. On our last visit to Rishikesh he was in Europe, so we only saw his plush ashram complete with sandalwood paneling—a luxury which, I might add, contradicts the ascetic nature of ashrams.

The timing is particularly auspicious. Every six years Hindu pilgrims visit Hardwar, near Rishikesh, to bathe in the Ganges. Hundreds of thousands of Hindus will converge here on the thirteenth for the Kumbh Mela festival. The Maharaja of Hardwar, who we met last year, told us about the festival and graciously invited us to be his guest. All available accommodations during the festival were booked years ago. He owns the property on the river bank at Har-ki-Pauri the most sacred bathing ghat.

Our small apartment overlooks the incredible conglomeration of people from all over India. Right in the middle of the chaos, a monkey slipped in a window and stole one of my sandals. When I chased him, I ended up in a police blockade that routed the lines of pilgrims twenty across—a veritable crush of humanity—away from the river. Two hours I circled trying to get back to the apartment. I never recovered my sandal.

The hot months we'll spend in Simla, where there are many camps of Tibetan refugees who need help. We can teach English

---

4. Today the site of the old Roerich estate in the Kullu Valley is home to the International Roerich Memorial Trust, an educational, scientific and cultural center honoring the Roerich family's accomplishments.

and whatever else we can offer in return for the Tibetans' wonderful friendship and continuous smiles.

Kailash Monastery

Dalhousie

Himachal Pradesh Sept 4, 1968

I celebrated my birthday by observing a symbolic fast. No food— only hot lemon water. The next day I enjoyed specials from the only super-like-market I've seen in India: peanut butter, lime marmalade and a tin of sardines from England.

Tarthang Tulku, our former Tibetan teacher and friend from Benares, has just left for New York! We haven't seen him for some months. Now we'll have to travel west to see him again.

My hair has been thinning and falling out. I don't know the cause. Maybe a lack of vitamin B 12 or iron. One Indian doctor recommended I rub linseed oil into my scalp daily.

Dalhousie receives over thirty feet of snow each winter. No food supplies arrive until the following spring. The market is almost shut down during the cold season. Soon we will return to the plains, the great vacuum of liberating chaos.

Kailash Monastery

Dalhousie

Himachal Pradesh

October 3, 1968

Already Dalhousie is unbelievably cold. The Himalayas, some forty or fifty miles north, are covered with fresh snowfall. Winds are icy blasts off the peaks. Keith plans to walk down from 8,000 feet to 1,000 feet—all the way to the plains. I'll travel by bus with the luggage, if the weather stays clear.

Last week the lamas had a three-day picnic. The feast celebrated a forty-day rainy season retreat which just ended. They performed puja, worship, every day and stayed indoors all forty days. The local Tibetan school teachers performed a historical drama featuring the Buddhist scholar, Atisha, who journeyed to Tibet to teach the dharma to the Tibetans. In the play, the contrast between the stark villages of India and the royal palace in Tibet was hilarious.

I'm painting many Tibetan motifs and figures. There is so much detail and so many delicate lines to perfect. Tibetan lamas study for years before they acquire such skill.

The resident Tibetan artist at the Kailash monastery will paint in the facial features of a Buddha image I painted. He empowers my painting with his blessing. Allen Ginsberg visited the monastery four years ago.

One of my paintings.

Me painting

Kashi

Benares

November 4, 1968

One week ago, I received your letter from July—three months late!

Did I mention that our room in Benares overlooks the Maharaja of Benares' grounds where his elephants graze on tree branches! We awake to the sound of elephants chomping wood outside our window.

I gained two pounds; my hair doesn't fall out so easily.

Kashi, ancient name for Benares

January 1969

Yesterday the great festival of the Goddess Sarasvati, the Goddess of the arts and music, marked the beginning of spring, even though it is only January. People erected many colorful cotton tents. Inside each tent a lovely image of the Goddess rode a swan and carried a sitar in one of her multiple hands. Lights, lamps, music, and incense filled shop windows and patios across the city. The presence of Sarasvati was celebrated at every temple. Today is bright and sunny—certainly very spring-like.

Happy to say my health is good and I enjoyed a winter free from even a cold which is unusual. Thank you so much for the vitamins. If I bundle up more, I stay warmer than last winter. Tights under my sari, woolen socks, leather shoes—not sandals—keep legs and feet toasty.

Ironically as my hair recovers and appears more abundant and beautiful, I consider shaving my head to put an end to thinking about my physical appearance all the time. On the other hand, I don't need to become a nun in order to lead a purifying and monastic life. A shaved head is only an external sign. If thoughts are pure, chances are my actions will be pure, also. All and Everything is in the Mind.

My first visit to a dentist in a long while wasn't difficult, painful, or expensive. What a relief. Except for underwear, I find most things I need. Most modern conveniences and necessities are available. But it's important to stay alert. Chaos, bewilderment and confusion threatens to disrupt daily life, especially in the crowded markets and city streets. If a wandering cow sits down in the middle of a street, traffic bypasses the obstacle. Can't nudge, push, coerce or shout at a reclining sacred bovine. Keep eyes open and maintain a sense of humor. A friend visited a dentist who operated a foot-pedaled drill!

I don't have any future plans except to continue my studies which are indispensable. Keith has a Tibetan teacher now. If I were to send some material for a skirt or dress for Peggy, what would be a good length in inches from the waist down? And Don, what size shirt? And Bill?

Sarnath

Uttar Pradesh

January 1969

This year the musicians Ali Akbar Khan and Ravi Shankar will perform at the annual Benares music festival. Have you heard, Ali Akbar Khan set up a music school in San Rafael? California appears to be a place where oriental culture can flourish.

In Bodh Gaya a few weeks ago, I had my first meeting with a Japanese Zazen priest. I practiced sitting meditation with him. The discipline of keeping a rigid back straight is a good one. When the body is immobile, the mind quiets. Focus shifts to the nostrils, the automatic inhalation and exhalation, the inevitable rising, falling of the rib cage, the rhythms of the blood pulsing through the veins. Thoughts rarely cease.

In Tibetan meditation the mind is channeled with an elaborate system of visualizations. To visualize the six-handed Mahakala, all aspects of his appearance are imagined: the red skin color, fierce stance, weapons in each of his six hands, background offerings, deities, clouds or flames. In some *sadhanas,* or meditations, an entire retinue of deities are brought to mind, like the one hundred medicine Buddhas. At any rate, my thoughts quieted down with the Zazen practice, but I felt helpless to control the wayward notions that inevitably crop up. Wandering mind. The elaborately dressed and adorned Tibetan deities with their assorted ornaments and retinues help the mind focus with so many specific details. There are Zazen centers in Palo Alto and San Francisco now.

Tarthang wrote from California. His teachings attract new students. He has plans to publish dharma books. California suits him. Keith has been working diligently with his teacher, Padma Wangyal, in Sarnath, translating prayers from a Nyingmapa prayer book. Tibetan Buddhism is divided into four sects: Gelugpa, Kargyudpa, Sakyapa and Nyingmapa—Tarthang is a Nyingmapa.

Varanasi

Uttar Pradesh

February 1969

My latest fascination is astrology. My horoscope was drawn up by my friend Maria. The signs in the zodiac and the influence of the planets point to an introverted inclination. Astrological speculation is interesting although there is no scientific rationale to explain it. The heavens are in constant flux. To attempt to interpret the various forces at play and relate them to my life and experience is intriguing. For the first time I located Leo in the night sky. As Leo moved towards the horizon, I wondered about the earliest people who first named the constellations and how the decision was made to locate and isolate particular groupings and not other groupings or clusters of stars. I see my own arrangements in the heavens; I'd like to redraw the constellations.

My newest tool is a Rapidograph—a fine pen used for drafting but also very useful in drawing, sketching, and fine calligraphy. My plans are not settled. Of course, my studies are indispensable.

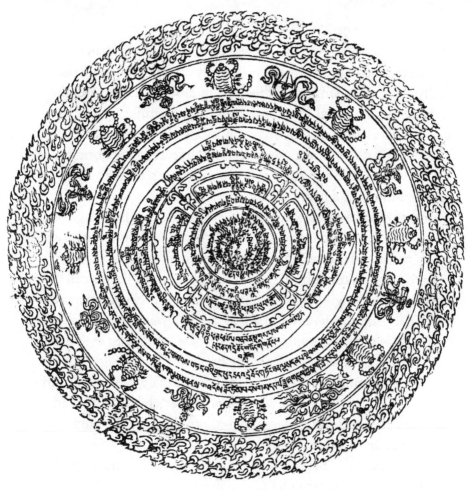

Auspicious mandala

Delhi

April 1969

How different Delhi is each time I visit. The influence of Western culture is evident in the hotels, restaurants and architecture.There is even a disco now. There are many more tourists this year. However fast and modern Delhi is becoming, I cannot stay in this noisy, crowded city for longer than two weeks.

We just saw the movie "Bullit" and marveled at the crisp, clear skies over the San Francisco bay. Exiting the cinema was surreal. The dust was so thick in pre-monsoon Delhi, all the buildings and even the trees were shades of soft brown, pink, and gray. Imagine gray trees. No blue or green whatsoever. Only after the rains will the sky really clear again. Until then the dry, hot desert winds scatter the dust and the heat becomes more and more intense until BOOM! the first clap of thunder heralds the sixty-day monsoon deluge. The rains are always dramatic. In the mountains I watch storm after storm move up the valley in slow motion at first until they arrive with blasts of rain, lightning, and heavy winds.

India is a climate of extremes: in temperature, in humidity, in geography.Even Delhi is an extreme distortion of modernity: twenty miles outside of the city the area is plagued by drought. The dry, rugged terrain cannot be irrigated. Ironically, the villagers call the rugged areas "jungle." But in reality, the land is rocky, sparsely covered in thorny shrubs and the soil is sand. I always pictured a "jungle" as a lush, overgrown tropical profusion of vines draped over banana trees with snakes dangling from the branches.

This is a period of transition. I'm sorry I can't give you an address just yet. We uprooted ourselves from a winter's hibernation and study. Where in the Himalayas we want to settle for the duration of the monsoon is still undecided.

My colloquial Tibetan is improving. Texts and manuscripts I copy are in a formal script which I taught myself. Ideally, I'd like to learn the other cursive script, too.

We met His Holiness Dudjom Jigdral Yeshe Dorje in Delhi last week. He is the head of the Nyingmapa sect of Tibetan Buddhist tradition which we study. The lotus born guru Rinpoche, or Padma Sambhava, is venerated in the Nyingma lineage. The other sects are Gelugpa (H.H. Dalai Lama is the head); Kargyupta (H.H. Karmapa is the head) and Sakya (Sakya Trizen is the head).

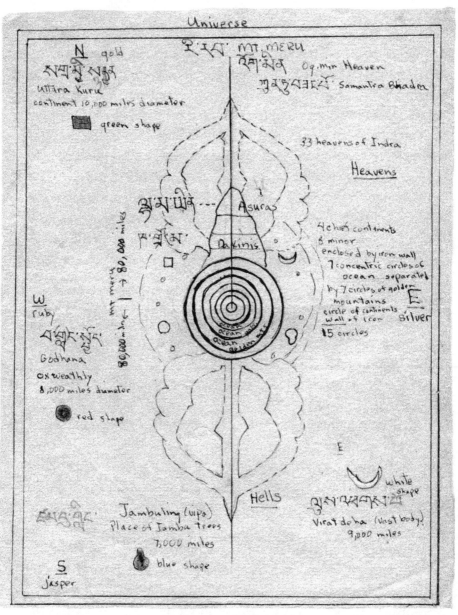

One of my drawings

Sarnath

April 1969

Just returned to Sarnath for a quick trip to close up the house and
get our things together for a move up to Darjeeling. Outside the temperature is over 100 degrees. Packing is exhausting. We had a nice
trip to Dharamsala and Delhi. In Almora, Keith and I consulted with
Lama Govinda on a particular translation of a Nyingmapa prayer. I
learned more about his theory of diagramming philosophical ideas.

Ah! The Ganges! Yesterday I had a glorious bath in the river. The
water is so refreshing and cool. No wonder the waters are sacred: a
refreshing liquid to cool hot bodies in the summer, to cure disease,
and ultimately to immerse the ashes of the dead. I say "bath" but
really everyone only dunks fully dressed and rinses off without soap.

I enjoy painting many traditional Tibetan motifs. Most are med-
itational diagrams that illustrate philosophical concepts (*yantras*).
The actual process of applying paint is so absorbing and satisfying,
a natural means to focus attention. My painting is a meditation. I try
not to become attached to any work I complete. Like a boat used to
cross a river—there is no reason to keep the boat once the journey is
completed.

There is an increasing number of westerners arriving in India. I
am not the only one in awe of this complex historical culture. The
ancient civilization never died. There are many ruins, but thankfully
the religion, arts and culture of India were never completely
destroyed. The continuity fascinates me. The latest archaeological
find reveals a civilization older than the one unearthed at Harappa.

Indians follow the American moon program they read about in
the newspapers. Village priests and local pundits pray for the safety
of the three astronauts and their space flight at huge public prayer
sessions. The way the Indians worry about the health and safety of
the astronauts is quite touching.

I'm reminded of the guard at the Libyan-Egyptian border.
He looked at my American passport and exclaimed "American!
Kennedy—American! Yes!!" He only knew two English words: "yes"

and "American" and the name of ex-president Kennedy, but it didn't stop him from expressing his passionate approval of Americans. He adores Kennedy, as do many villagers in Asia. At least Americans are in favor these days.

Darjeeling
June 1969

I'm so glad you met Tarthang Tulku and his wife in San Francisco. Give him our best wishes if you see him again. Is he giving talks on Buddhism?

Last September ten inches of rain fell every day for three consecutive days. Scores of landslides killed hundreds of people. The Darjeeling area of north east India is the wettest in the country. Many tulkus, reincarnated lamas, live here.I have many opportunities to practice my Tibetan. My painting work continues as I copy mantras in circular diagrams and paint many of the deities.

On the full moon we walked to a nearby peak, about 9,000 feet above sea level, and saw the bright orange moon set as the golden sun rose over the Himalayan peaks. The sun rose at 4:00 a.m. The Tibetans celebrated the last full moon day as the Buddha's birthday. They chanted at many prayer ceremonies before feasting and dancing.

We had a full week of clear skies. Our bungalow is actually a duplex which we share with Kanjur Rimpoche and his family. His son, Padma Wangyal, is Keith's Tibetan teacher. The house sits on a ridge facing the lovely peak of Kanchenjunga. The view is awesome when the clouds clear. We might trek inside the Nepalese border if the rains hold off.

P.S. Can you smell this scent? (XXX) I soaked this spot with musk which comes, I'm told, from the liver of a deer. The scent is much richer than sandalwood, don't you think?

c/o Postmaster
Darjeeling
West Bengal
July 1969

We walked seventeen miles yesterday. From Darjeeling we
descended a forested ridge and passed through many tea estates.
We crossed the Teesta river at the bottom and climbed up a ridge to
Kalimpong. From 7,500 feet down to 3,000 feet and up again to 6,000
feet. My feet are very tender today.

Yesterday we visited Yogi Chen, a Chinese Buddhist who settled
in India. He writes and publishes many booklets on various aspects
of Buddhism—especially Vajrayana. When he was in China thirty
years ago, he dreamed of a particular formation of mountains that
opened their arms to protect him. He spotted the same mountain
formation he dreamed of in the village of Kalimpong so he decided
to stay and build a retreat hut.

"The mountains opened their arms to protect me," he demonstrated. "They invited me to stay. So, I stayed. I'm still here," he
chuckled with his big Buddha belly.

He hasn't left his room for twenty years! I will send you a few of
his pamphlets. I brought him an offering of homemade fudge. He
smiled broadly and ate three pieces one after the other.

Darjeeling is lively. A crispness electrifies the air and the people. I
attended a special prayer ceremony and initiation last week. Usually
these rituals are kept secret, but we were allowed to attend. The
lamas wore beautiful silken robes and danced with masks of angry,
wrathful gods. Their movements are very stylized. At times, their
voices let loose an eerie yodeling that seemed to drift out across the
vast Himalayan valleys. The Tibetans are so at home here. Many own
land and houses. They are not refugees, in other words, broken in
spirit and pocketbook like the refugees in camps in India.

Please understand that my letters only relate some of my travel
experiences, especially those of a physical nature: where I traveled,

what I visited, what interests me, what I'm studying. What I feel strongest about and what I really want to relay is impossible to express. What I am trying to accomplish by means of my physical body is to generate, recognize, and live the feelings of love and compassion.

P.S. My new Tibetan name is: Lhamo Saykyi which means God Woman Life Happy, or Goddess of Happy Life.

Monk giving a ritual offering.

Darjeeling,
West Bengal
Mid-monsoon, 1969

I borrowed a camera from Sherab Tharchin, a friend, and if I can get it to work, I'd love to send you some photos. The photo of the Tibetan woman on the front of this postcard shows a rich array of turquoise, amber, and coral jewelry. She only wears her complex headdress, three feet wide and a foot high(!), on rare occasions.

Darjeeling
July 29, 1969

Today I sent a parcel of the finest hill grown Darjeeling tea via sea mail, so you can expect it in three months. A long time, I know, but the company is well established, and they ship worldwide. Darjeeling is my favorite tea. To retain the distinct flavor, the best buds are picked and dried in the fall, stored in tins and carefully packed in wooden boxes for shipping. Connoisseurs can distinguish between the flavors of different high-altitude teas.

There are many varieties of tea to choose from. At the market, burlap bags full of loose tea are arranged in rows. To smell the aroma, I cup a small amount between my palms and exhale warm air onto the leaves to release the scent. Indians drink tea like water, that is, all day long. Since the tea is boiled, the chances of catching a bug are less than if I drink the local untreated water. So, I drink many cups a day also.

The British planted many tea plantations or estates in the foothills of the Himalayas and introduced to the continent the tea drinking habit. Tibetans add rancid yak butter (like blue cheese), milk from a yak, or dri, and salt, then churn the mixture into a warm broth which takes the chill off in cold weather.

Please write to me c/o American Express, Delhi. We'll visit Orissa on the Bay of Bengal first.

Puri

Orissa state

August 20, 1969

A friend, John Hardy, invited us to visit his farm in Orissa near the ocean on the Bay of Bengal south of Calcutta. The land was a former ashram or Hindu rural community. An American Tibetan scholar, W. Evans-Wentz, who actually studied at Stanford, once lived in the crumbling meditation hut.

I walked to the nearest tiny shop, four miles away but only rice, kerosene, and potatoes were available there. My arrival excited the women and girls in the village. They scurried to surround me. Where are my bangles, they wanted to know? Why didn't I wear bangles on my wrist? Married women always wear bangles.

The women wondered if I came from North India where they heard some Kashmiris have blue eyes. They'd never heard of America. A village man sells stamps from the porch of his mud bungalow—that's the post office. I walked eight miles to hand-carry and post this letter and return home—after briefly getting lost in a cashew nut forest.

The farm is a twenty-acre parcel planted with cashew nut trees, pineapples, coconuts, lemons, and mangos. John grows tapioca which is like a sweet potato root. The property is rimmed by a river, the ocean half a mile away and sandy dunes on the other two sides. To get anything to grow is a miracle in this sandy soil.

John built the bamboo house. The roof is thatch; walls are mud. The dwelling is elevated six feet above ground in case the river floods. He married a Tibetan woman. They live with their two sons and farm the land. Drinking water comes from pools dug in the sand. The water table is only six feet.

The ocean is terrific. How many years since I swam in an ocean! Too many. Probably Juhu Beach in Bombay was the last time, three years ago. Curiously I'm the only one who swims in the ocean. Indians just do not swim. In Puri, a large city sixteen miles to the south, Indian "lifeguards" earn a living standing in the waves to hold hands with timid villagers who want to take a ritual dip in the ocean. The lifeguards have their hands full clinging to the nervous, weak, and extremely thin pilgrims who might easily be swept out to sea.

There is a very strong undertow where I swim. Fortunately, the pull is parallel to the shore...until the mouth of the river meets the sea and the water and current then push offshore in one tremendous thrust.

Luckily, I placed my towel on the beach last week before I went swimming. Otherwise there was no marker to tell me where I entered the water. Within minutes the towel was way down the beach. That towel saved my life! I'm careful now and wade more than swim.

Not four miles from the farm is an enormous Sun Temple built on the sea and abandoned to the sun. The sea has receded two miles since the Konarak temple was constructed in the shape of an enormous chariot of Surya, the Sun God. The walls are covered with erotic sculptures. The sun, the sea, and the temple of worship all create a mystical atmosphere. Hot sun, sea breezes, and salt water invigorate me. Keith's fortitude, on the other hand, varies in different climates. The English tend to wilt in the sun.

I remember the sun pyramids I visited in Mexico, Egypt, and a sun temple by the sea in Greece.

S 15/131 A Mawaiya Road
Sarnath, U.P.

September 1969

I traveled north from Puri to Benares with John and his family. Tsewang, John's Tibetan wife, worries about the plight of her people in India. Refugees have many obstacles to overcome. There is some aid available to them. Many English organizations sponsor the construction of new buildings: monasteries and nunneries as well as schools for young lamas.

For the journey we reserved second-class seats on the train, but in the middle of nowhere nomads forced the windows open and stormed in. There was no stopping them in the chaos. The car was soon packed. Some passengers stretched out on the overhead luggage racks and promptly fell fast asleep!

We were the only passengers with tickets. Ticket collectors, by the way, are rare. The cars fill up—not only the seats, but the aisles, too. Ticket collectors would have an impossible time walking through the crowded cars. Some railway stations post signs: "Ticketless Travel is a Social Evil." But enforcing ticketed travel is an overwhelming task.

Miraculously the trains keep running.

We moved into a house we share with John and family about three-quarters of a mile from the market in Sarnath, a village outside of Benares. The walls are stucco. Keith and I live upstairs. The yard is surrounded by thick, high walls where wild peacocks perch and sometimes screech in the night. John's radio picks up China, Russia, Ceylon, Indonesia, Australia, and even broadcasts from Germany. We listen to the radio some nights. I haven't seen a television except one in a storefront in Delhi a few months ago. A street crowd of Indians stood transfixed, watching astronauts in space suits clomp around on the moon. Phone service is very rare or nonexistent in the villages where we travel. We're lucky if we have any electricity.

Monks' procession

Sarnath

October 1969

We spent our first winter in India in Sarnath. Since that time there are
twice as many tourists and antiquity shops. Although there are still no
hotels, all of the *dharamsalas* (pilgrim hostels) are filled with Tibetan
refugees. The Jain, Ceylonese, Burmese, and Chinese temples all house
Tibetans. In addition, the Tibetan monastery is crowded with lamas
who study at the new Institute for Higher Tibetan Studies.

His Holiness, the Dalai Lama, is expected to visit in a few days.
My conversational Tibetan is improving with more contacts with
Tibetans.

Sarnath

November 24, 1969

Yesterday six lamas in a Buddhist procession around the Deer Park in
Sarnath, carried the fragile relics of the Buddha, encased in a miniature golden stupa. Monks blew twelve-foot Tibetan wood and silver
trumpets and beat drums to accompany monks who chanted prayers.
Satisfaction comes to those who open their eyes to see the amazing
world we all live in. To understand each other we need to listen,
watch, and share. I try to follow my heart.

To walk a foot-worn trail through a forest of trees and wildflowers;
to bathe in a river next to a herd of water buffalos; to feel the surf
pounding through my body or to inhale blustering Himalayan
rain-laden clouds—these experiences invigorate and amaze me.

Sarnath

February 12, 1970

For Tibetan New Year, John brewed his own rice beer. The Tibetan
cook at the village restaurant prepared deep-fried twisted bread

sticks and served homemade rice wine. Tibetan men, after consuming *chang* or rice beer, danced in front of the monastery while the women sang and clapped hands.

Another festival in Benares celebrated the Hindu first day of spring, already. I took an early morning dip in the Ganges along with crowds of people—a crazy, temple bell-clanging, chaotic scene—water buffalos stampeded to the water and thousands of pilgrims splashed prayers to the deities of the four directions.

Last night all the images of Sarasvati were carried through the alleyways, down to the river where they were immersed in the water.

What is the cabin in Portola Valley like? I can't remember much about it. Is there a lot of land, woods, and a creek nearby? You mentioned Ken Kesey, your tenant in Portola. How long has he lived there? Does he farm or raise animals?

When I cook with Indian spices, I wonder how they compare to western spices. Is there a book on spices, their sources, and use in cooking? I miss high school visits to Kepler's where I bought so many great books by Alan Watts, and the Chinese poets, Tu Fu and Wang Wei.

When we visited Yogi Chen in Kalimpong he showed us a letter from Gary Snyder describing the property he purchased in the Sierra Nevada mountains. It sounds lovely. I'd like to visit him there one day.

Remember the report I wrote in high school on Gandhi's vegetarianism? He founded a string of Gandhi emporiums, a group of regional cooperative shops called Khadi Ashrams that feature handiwork and crafts from all over India. At one Khadi Ashram in Manali I bought a thick wool blanket and a glass jar of Kullu wildflower honey, good products.

To publicize the movement to recognize the importance of native handicrafts, Gandhi is often pictured behind a spinning wheel. *Khadi* is the name of the hand-spun fabric sold in the Khadi Ashrams. Keith wears handwoven cotton *khadi kurta* shirts. To write down my dreams I stitched a notebook out of interesting handmade paper I bought at one of the Gandhi emporiums. Beautiful marbled paper decorates the cover.

Sarnath
February 27, 1970

The hot season is almost here again. Before we resettle for the summer, a quick visit to Dharamsala. His Holiness will perform the *Kalachakra* initiation for the first time outside of Tibet. Formerly, he would only perform this ceremony once in his lifetime. Since we haven't been to Dharamsala for two and a half years, we look forward to another pleasant visit to the Kangra Valley and the western Himalayas.

I met an anthropologist, Robert Gross, a friend of my high school buddy Diana. He's researching Hindu sadhus for his dissertation at the University of California, Berkeley. India is always disorienting at first; the change in the standard of living and mysterious cultural customs are difficult to understand. Luckily Robert is familiar with Hindi and knows a great deal about the Hindu religion and culture from his studies. Once he becomes adjusted to India his studies will flourish.

Last week I splurged on a recently republished Tibetan-Sanskrit-English Dictionary. It has been unavailable for a number of years.

I hope everyone is in perfect health and peacefully enjoying the spontaneously arising nature of self-contained ecstasy.

Delhi
March 3, 1970

The mail clerk at the American Express said he received a letter requesting my mail be forwarded elsewhere. I suspect this is an alibi. I will inform the manager. This may explain why I received the Christmas parcel so late—almost Easter, in fact. I'm grateful it arrived. What a pleasant surprise. Thank you so much!

There are many foreign students in Delhi who combine travel with studying Indian music and philosophy. Like me, many live frugally. They avoid material possessions like cars, televisions, and stereos in order to visit India and learn the ancient ways. When they return to the west some plan to teach what they learned here—various eastern traditions like yoga, meditation, and Indian dance. The Indians, on the other hand, are the opposite. They're interested in modernizing and buying televisions, refrigerators, and motorized vehicles.

The longer I stay in India, the more my awareness and understanding broadens. It's easier to see myself more objectively after I gain some knowledge and experience of another culture. Emotions like joy or sorrow persist in every culture. I exist on a worldly plane and to deny this existence would be useless and false. I strive not to cling to the poisons of human nature i.e. greed, lust, jealousy. With meditation I hope to eliminate unpleasant thoughts—or, at least learn not to cling to them.

Samsara is Existence is Nirvana is Perfection is Now & Here.

The warm tights are great. Now all I need now is—just kidding! Desire is endless, isn't it? No matter how much or how little we have, we always crave more. Take food, for instance, a daily necessity. We can't live without eating. No sooner do we satisfy one craving, then another comes to mind.

Never mind these scattered thoughts penned on my last pre-stamped aerogram. It's impossible to erase the ink and begin again. I just want to thank you so much for the lovely gifts.

Delhi

March 15, 1970

Do you like this beautiful handmade paper I purchased in one of the Gandhi Ashram stores? The rice paper is actually made from the lokta plant in Nepal. Other papers are made from silk and bamboo. Really exquisite.

My friend Turina gave me a pair of knee length suede boots. I've always wanted a pair. They're perfect with the tights to wear in the mountains. We're on our way to Dharamsala to receive teachings from H.H. the Dalai Lama. Many thousands of Tibetans travel from all over the Himalayas to attend the ceremonies which haven't been given since His Holiness resided in his Potala Palace in Lhasa eleven years ago. We're very excited.

After I visit my teachers in Darjeeling, I'll travel to Nepal to make some prints from wood blocks of carved Buddha and deities from a Tibetan monastery in Nepal. The designs are unique, attractive, and unavailable except from monastic libraries. I painted one dragon and it turned out very well.

Please, can I trouble you again? A friend just received a manila sealed envelope Registered Mail, Air Delivery, sent to American Express, New Delhi. Inside, a Parker pen in a box.

I would love some Japanese brushes to paint with. Remember my brush painting class on channel 9? Four Japanese brushes of the smallest size possible and one black Japanese sumi ink stick would be wonderful. The small size will accommodate the detailed style of the Tibetan script. I have a Rapidograph, but strokes made with a brush would be much better. Please forgive all my requests. I appreciate everything you've done for me. If it's not too much trouble, new brushes would help with my calligraphy work. Thanks so much.

Living in a foreign country far from home is difficult. Even though there are many hardships to face every day I still feel lucky to be here in this exciting time. It is sad that the Tibetans had to flee their homeland, but the teachers are now available for the first time outside of Tibet.

The future holds great prospects. Being a woman, I'd like to experience the joy of motherhood—a joy you, Mother, have experienced six times.

Deer are one of the most peace-loving animals. They appear in many Buddhist paintings. The mural in the temple at the Deer Park in Sarnath features many deer. The way you describe the ranch near the ocean sounds like a perfect place for a retreat. All life is a retreat so what better place for a home?

I love this quote from Basho, a Japanese poet of the seventeenth century: "Every day is a journey and the journey itself home."

Calcutta
West Bengal
April 6, 1970

I had a nice plane ride from Siligiri to Calcutta where I hope to renew my visa. With a student discount the flight cost only five dollars! Such is India. But prices are rising steadily from two years ago. I'm staying with Michal Abrams, a friend I knew in Dalhousie. We're going to the local Chinese quarter to purchase some jasmine tea imported from Hong Kong.

Lama Kalu invited me to paint a Tibetan mural on the new wall of his expanded shrine room at the monastery in Sonada, West Bengal. There are so many manifestations of peaceful and wrathful deities and images of scenes from the life of the Buddha to depict. I'm thrilled and consequently need to return to Darjeeling quickly.

Also near Sonada, in the village of Ghoom, there will be an annual ritual ceremony I want to attend. Calcutta weather is sticky and medium hot, but I enjoy visiting friends, shopping, and catching a matinee or two—a luxury for me not available in village India. The main Darjeeling market reminds me of an indoor Mexican market where every kind of item is available in one of dozens of shops under a huge roof.

I wonder if you could get a book for me, please? *Magic Squares and Cubes*, W.S. Andrews, 419 pages, 754 diagrams, paperbound, $1.85 from Dover Publications, Inc. 180 Varick Street, NY 14, NY. Let me confirm my address first though. Maybe you could let me know if it's available. The Hindu temple attached to our room at the Niranjani Akara at Shivala ghat in Benares has a lovely brass door incised with numbers arranged in magical squares. I'm interested in researching European use of magic squares. A magic square appears in one of Albrecht Durer's etchings from the fifteenth century.

c/o American Express
New Delhi India

April 23, 1970

Happy Birthday, Mother! A thousand flowers and blessings to you.
May you enjoy the sublime pleasure of watching, witnessing the
flow of life. I would love to spend the day with you. I look forward to
when that happens. Soon I hope.

It snowed in Dharamsala on one of the days of the Kalachakra ceremony. Oddly the next day Tibetans suffered from sunburn and sunstroke
as the ceremony was outdoors and lasted a good ten hours non-stop.

Thank you so much for the Japanese paint brushes! I haven't tried
them yet but as soon as I get a chance I will use the brush and ink on
some rice paper, the traditional handmade paper from Nepal.

I'm staying with Lynn Weinberger, a photographer working for
UNICEF. Previously she and her husband were in the Peace Corps.
The luxury of using modern conveniences is a welcome change. I
look forward to the day when I can acquire a retreat, even a log cabin,
in the high mountains.

Sometimes I feel like a pioneer risking the wilds and stomping
over new territory. Living in luxury or camping out both have
attractive qualities. The coastal area of Northern California is so
beautiful. A retreat near the ocean would provide a quiet atmosphere
for contemplation and reflective thinking and it would also be close
enough—closer than India—to maintain connections with friends
and the cultural opportunities of Berkeley or San Francisco.

I don't know if you can say my meditation has improved or if it's
a result of conquering or subduing fears and doubts or whatever, but
I certainly float lightly and enjoy life so much in India now. I have so
many more friends than when we first arrived. I understand more
about the complexities of Indian society and customs. Nothing to
protest; nothing to prove. Just enjoy the flow of karma with friends.
Thank you again for the paint brushes. The speed and efficiency of
air mail is incredible. The package wasn't even opened! May life
continue to reward you with peace and happiness.

Sonada
West Bengal
May 17, 1970

I rent a room in Sonada near my teacher Kalu Rinpoche's gompa. I stay here a few nights a week. Yesterday we celebrated a ceremony that marked the beginning of a new three-year, three-month, three-day retreat for thirteen lamas who will practice intense meditation in sealed rooms. Their living conditions are very austere. The monks never leave the retreat. They sit most of the day in wooden boxes built according to the specific measurement of each monk as he sits, legs crossed, in the posture of meditation.

Historically the isolated training provided essential meditative experience for many lamas. Recently after so many Tibetan refugees fled their homeland, the strict practice had been discontinued. Only a few higher lamas like Kalu Rinpoche are capable of instructing the monks.

Lama Kalu is very considerate of his western students who fit into a specific category in the spiritual organization of the monastic community.

It was prophesized that Tibet would be invaded, and it was, by the Chinese. Another prophecy claims the dharma will spread to the west where it will flourish.

Buddha dharma is without form in the purest essence. It's a way of living, of daily practice, and a way of guiding thoughts. The biggest change is internal. To live in a foreign land, the Buddha said, enables one to gain spiritual experience far from friends, family, and material possessions. These conditions are good for meditation. I agree.

Darjeeling
West Bengal
June 13, 1970

How wonderful the ranch sounds. A country retreat is really a good cure for stress, tension, and frustrations. Better than any pills a doctor prescribes. Where is the location? Is Bodega Bay on the ocean? How far north of San Francisco is it?

We saw "Flight to Doomsday" last night, a movie that involves a bomb placed on an airliner. The acting was awful. Actors panicked and shouted at each other. The film depressed me. Americans are terrified of death and aging. The young have no respect for their elders. This is sad. So unlike Asia where parents are honored. Elders should realize the importance of wisdom and experience. I feel I can confide in you my intimate reflections. I don't normally talk about these things.

As for death, one must accept the ultimate fact that life is impermanent. Every living being ultimately dies.

Rain is falling—I must run and collect my hand-washed clothes stretched out over bushes to dry in the garden.

c/o Sun Building
Dhanbhaduar Road (next door to Tenzing Norgay's house)
Darjeeling, WB
July 1970

The monsoon this year is relatively mild. Even though the rainfall isn't as heavy as usual, dampness still penetrates everything. Colorful blue and green molds grow on the walls and on leather shoes and belts. I must keep flour and lentils in air-tight containers or else it spoils and turns green.

Keith went to Calcutta to find a printer for his first book of Tibetan prayers he translated into English. He found a good printer who can finish the job in six to eight weeks, but his return was delayed two days because of the complete shutdown of all transportation. Workers went on strike. Perhaps you read about it?

Another sign that the monsoon is lighter this year—there have been no major landslides. As I write I hear the whistle of the Darjeeling Himalayan railroad that ascends from the plains in Siligiri up to 6,000 feet. What a charming, small blue train that chugs along, negotiating the constant switchbacks that enable it to climb up the steep mountain range. It has a toy-like appearance. Bill would love it. We rode on it once, but it took twice as long as a jeep ride. The jeep drivers shift into neutral and coast down the mountain to save gas.

I cooked bamboo shoots last night—my first time. Not sure if they're a delicacy or not but we enjoyed the thick radish-like roots sliced and added to a vegetable stir-fry.

Darjeeling
July 11, 1970

Keith and I just returned from a nice visit to Kalimpong near the border with Sikkhim, a tiny Himalayan kingdom. We went with some friends from Minneapolis, who use their Tibetan names now: Sonam Chutso, Sherab Tharchin, and his mother, Mrs. Ebin. I'll send his mother's telephone number. She has some slides of our trip and will be happy to chat with you about our life in Darjeeling.

We visited with Yogi Chen again. He is planning a move to Berkeley soon. Every time a friend leaves for the west I get a pang of sadness. I'd love to return soon and look forward to the day I do return, but my studies here are more important for now. I'm reading John Blofeld's *The Way of Power* which describes the vajrayana Buddhist tradition.

Yesterday I had a glorious sunbath in the midst of the monsoon. Unusual. Cloud-covered skies gave way to deep clear indigo blue. Crystal sparkling Mt. Kachenjunga beamed in the distance. Sunshine sparkled on trees and grass. The field outside our cottage sprang to life with insects wallowing in the warm rays. All the mold should disappear from my clothes and the walls before long. I keep busy with the small tasks of daily life: cooking, painting, sewing.

Sun Building
Darjeeling
July 25, 1970

That's great the Tibetan carpets arrived via sea mail after three months! The dragon and phoenix design and the geometric manda-las are my favorites.

Please Mom, don't despair, you've been so wonderful and good and kind, and I know how long I've been away. Five years is a really long time. Believe me, I'd love to come home but it isn't the right time yet. What we're doing involves working closely with the few amazing Tibetan elders who have the knowledge and compassion to teach. Here is the only place where they live outside of Tibet.

The ranch sounds great. Please have faith and patience. I will return to the west as soon as I feel I'm ready. In the near future. Rest assured, before long I'll be with you all again. This August I'll turn 24.

Think of my absence this way: if I'm lucky I might live to the age of 75. If you divide 75 by 5 (representing my five years absence) the result is that only $1/5$ of my life was spent away from home. This sounds like a long time but not if you consider the bigger picture. And the five years were well spent studying Asian arts that aren't taught in the west.

Sun Building
Darjeeling
August 22, 1970

To begin an unusual approach to the customary birthday wish list—I send all my warmth and appreciation and fond loving thoughts to both of you, my parents, who so kindly bore all the difficulties of raising me and caring for my physical and spiritual development. This birthday I have special thoughts about thanking you both for everything and all things beyond numeration. All the presents and wishes should go to you both. My deepest feelings and infinite love I extend to you. Happy Birthday!

Keith gave me a lovely pashmina shawl which is so soft, like cashmere, made from the fine neck hairs of Himalayan sheep in Kashmir, India. Tonight we'll celebrate with dinner and cake with friends at the Windamere, a pukka English style hotel. The bar at the Windamere is where Hope Cooke, the American-born queen of Sikkhim, the locals claim, met her future husband. My friend Michal Abrams is visiting.

Another matter I need to inform you about. I am having a little trouble with the local authorities concerning my visa status. Keith being British is exempt since India is a Commonwealth country and British citizens can travel freely within the Commonwealth. My last visa expired and hasn't been renewed yet. I must stay in Darjeeling until the case is investigated. There is no need for alarm. It may involve a court case which should prove interesting, and hopefully not too expensive. The silver lining is that I can stay here for a few months without a permit. Darjeeling is a "sensitive area" near the Chinese border. Visitors need special permits in addition to their current visas.

c/o Mr. Tenzing Norgay
Dhanbhaduar Road Darjeeling
September 11, 1970

My tentative plan is to travel to Kathmandu in October for the winter. Then in the spring I'm thinking of returning. If you could, please send the book immediately by sea mail to me c/o Visitors Mail, American Embassy, Kathmandu. I'm having warm clothes made as the winter is quite cold there. A long-sleeved lined woolen *chuba*, a Tibetan type of robe the men and women wear, is warm and thick like a long bathrobe. My visa situation is still pending.

I moved next door into the house of Tenzing Norgay, the Sherpa mountain climber who first climbed Mt. Everest with Edmund Hillary. He is a very happy man and very nice. His love for the mountains is inspiring. Maybe you can read a book about him called, *Tiger of the Snows*, that describes the ascent of Mt. Everest.

The house is more comfortable with a bathtub and telephone although I don't need a phone. Who would I call? None of my friends have a telephone. A few lamas do but they don't use the phone either.

A cold, rainy week here.

All knowledge comes from within. Natural surroundings let the essence of peace flow from within. Your visit to the country sounds very nice, close to nature and wild animals. A country retreat has good potential, perfect for anyone who seeks solitude and a contemplative life.

I've been reading Sufi poetry lately. I still enjoy haiku with the simple but truthful epiphanies of spirit. *The Way of the Sufi* by Idries Shah has charming stories.

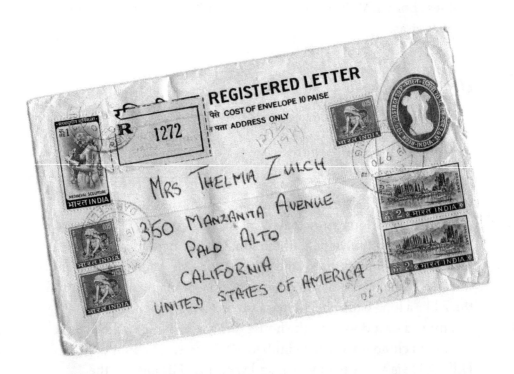

c/o Tenzing Norgay
Dhanbhadaur Road
Darjeeling
September 16, 1970

Enclosing some photos. I hope they arrive in good condition.

I photographed Keith before and after his transformation. He shaved his head, took a layman's vow to study the dharma, and now wears Tibetan robes instead of western clothes. Here he's sitting at the gravesite of an early explorer, the Hungarian Alexander Csoma de Koros, one of the first Tibetan scholars who compiled the first Tibetan Dictionary. He died of malaria in Darjeeling in 1842—over 120 years ago—on his way back to Tibet. The small stupa monument commemorates his life.

Another picture is of Kalu Rinpoche, who resides in the monastery in Sonada where I painted the mural in the shrine room.

We're still besieged by the monsoon here. A long five months. Any day I'm expecting the rains to cease and give way to the clearest blue skies and brilliant white peaks rising above Sikkim.

I'm finishing a mandala painting in the mountain hermitage of Chatral Sangye Dorje Rinpoche. When I saw the painting in his study on a recent visit, I was immediately inspired. It is very unusual. I asked permission to copy the Tara mandala and was thrilled when the reclusive lama said I could.

Every morning I hop on a jeep shuttle and ride to his hermitage in Ghoom, about ten kilometers away. I walk up a rugged mountain trail to his compound. Since there are many Tibetan mantras and letters in the diagrammatic painting, Chatral Sangye Dorje Rinpoche volunteered to locate the passages from texts in old manuscripts from his library. This helps a lot as I can copy directly from the original text—the letters are bigger and easier to decipher. In painting Tibetan iconographic images, it is essential to avoid any mistakes however small.

Chatral Rinpoche, although a reclusive man, has a great sense of humor. He's the only Tibetan I know who is a vegetarian. Every month he travels from his hermitage down to the plains. He purchases live fish from the local market. Then an attendant rows him out to the middle of the river and he releases the fish, chanting good luck prayers for the long life of each fish. He would never harm or kill any animal or insect. The compassionate act of freeing caged animals, including birds, is considered very honorable and auspicious.

c/o Visitors Mail
US Embassy
Kathmandu
October 1970

A whirlwind surrounds me. The District Commissioner, who serves as magistrate, will drop the charges that I overstayed my visa provided that I "Quit India" within seven days. With some reluctance I agreed.

The phrase "Quit India" strikes me as peculiar and rings of futility. In reality I've reached the culmination of four years of intense study.

Lama Kalu will write a letter to Sabchu Rinpoche, Kargyupa Lama at the Svayambhunath gompa. I will hand carry the letter which will serve as my introduction into the community. It was a Tibetan custom to hand carry letters in Tibet where there was no mail or telephone service.

I completed the mandala which I have been working on for over a month. Chatral Sangye Dorje Rinpoche wrote a note asking H.H. Dudjom Jigdral Yeshe Dorje, the head of the Nyingmapa sect, to empower the painting, which he did. He was very impressed with my work. There are many Tibetan words and prayers surrounding the mandala. He complimented my calligraphy—thanks again for sending those great brushes! They are perfect to use for my calligraphy work.

My Muslim tailor finished two woolen jumpers to wear this winter in Kathmandu. Things fall into place. Keith will stay here with his teacher to finalize his book distribution. Although a return to India and especially Darjeeling would be unlikely, I'm not sad to leave.

Departures anticipate loss of friends but promise the excitement of new situations, friendships, and beginnings.

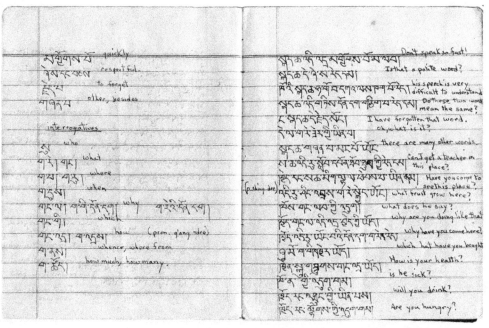

Pages from my calligraphy excercise book

TWO

A Room
in
Kathmandu

c/o Visitors Mail
US Embassy
Kathmandu, Nepal
November 1970

I settled into a room in Kathmandu, the capital city of Nepal. Two friends live nearby. The only furniture is a wood-plank bed with a cotton mattress, a wooden chair, and a small table I use for a desk. One of my prized Tibetan carpets—actually a saddle carpet for a horse or a yak—drapes over the bed. There is no central heat but if I light a fire in the small fireplace, the room heats up quickly. My morning routine begins with a cold-water shower followed by a pot of hot chai.

I plan to get the Tara mandala I painted in Darjeeling framed to hang on the wall. For now, my woodblock print collection and the mandala are rolled up and stacked in a corner of the room. On a small ledge a gold-plated Buddha statue—a gift from Harold Talbot, a good friend in Darjeeling who traveled with Thomas Merton during his travels around India and Darjeeling.

Interesting that Thomas Merton visited with Chatral Sangye Dorje Rinpoche in his hermitage during the time I painted the Tara mandala. To think I may have passed Thomas Merton on that small mountain path to the hermitage. I was so close to meeting him.

I presented my letter of introduction from Kalu Rinpoche to Sabchu Rinpoche at the Svayambhunath monastery, also known as the Monkey Temple since the hill outside of town is populated by wild monkeys. The rinpoche welcomed me to his gompa and assigned me a personal teacher. I was thrilled when Pecham, my new teacher, found a manuscript of the songs of the early Indian yogi and poet Saraha, who I want to study. We'll begin translating the poems next week.

An accomplished Tibetan artist, Wangyal, from the northern Nepalese border region of Dolpo, lives nearby and shares a house with William, an American scholar researching Tibetan ritual. I enjoy

Pecham

watching Wangyal learn western customs as I try to learn his eastern ones.

I met William when I visited Sarnath last year with Keith. He has studied in India and Nepal on a Fulbright fellowship for a number of years. His focus is on a particular deity, Mahakala. He has been very helpful introducing me to the best cafes and markets.

c/o Visitors Mail
US Embassy
Kathmandu
early December 1970

The city of Kathmandu has amazing architecture. When I walk the alleys between the intricately carved medieval wood buildings I feel like I stepped back in history. Spice shops sell dried turmeric and curry powders, herbs and seeds in colorful glass jars. Burlap bags filled with whole grain white rice, whole wheat flour, yellow, pink and brown lentils crowd the closet-like shops that line the alley. Incense wafts through the streets especially in the early morning when a blanket-like winter fog hovers in the crisp morning air.

My colloquial Tibetan is improving quickly since I'm able to practice with both Wangyal and William. My facility with spoken Tibetan helps me communicate with my teacher Pecham. All of my teachers have been from the area of Kham in the far eastern region of Tibet, a wild, rugged place.

The Nepalese are very skilled craftsmen and craftswomen. The temples, the Hindu and Buddhist statuary, the jewelry and the fabrics are handloomed or block printed. The women wear the family's wealth sculpted into ornate gold and silver ornaments.

I purchased a variety of handloomed silks from a shop. The fabric is not sheer silk but of a sturdier texture woven with heavier thread. A number of the Tibetan monks sew colorful brocade banners that hang in the gompas. Interesting to discover an illustration in one of Pecham's antique manuscripts of a monk's robe made from odd squares and rectangular patches stitched together. It seems as if the Tibetan patchwork tradition predates American patchwork quilts. The women wear long-sleeved blouses that tie in the front. For winter they wear blouses made from three layers of the same light cotton, but cotton batting is inserted between two layers for extra warmth.

c/o Visitors Mail
US Embassy
Kathmandu
December 24, 1970

Tonight is Christmas Eve. I'll join some friends for a potluck later. I'll make an exotic fruit salad with shreds of fresh coconut, mandarin orange slices, and pieces of a wonderful Nepali fruit called *nashpati*, which is a cross between a crisp pear and an apple. To top off the salad, I'll open a tin of mangos to decorate the top—they are out of season now. When I described the dish I'd bring—the potluck is at William and Wangyal's home—William remembered a Christmas fruitcake I prepared in Sarnath last year. I steamed the batter for two cakes in coffee tins set in a pan of boiling water on my kerosene stove. He fondly remembers that cake.

I send my Season's Greetings to everyone. May you have a wonderful holiday season.

This season is one of reflection for me. I cannot enjoy the holiday season without thinking about the nature of joy and celebration. Of course, I miss all of you, my family, and the opportunity to share festivities with you.

The innocent, joyful holiday expectations I had as a child are gone. Deeper thoughts and concerns weigh heavily. There is nothing wrong with reflection—that being one gift I possess. The mind, though, can be burdensome.

Kathmandu

December 31, 1970

I send every wish for a joyful holiday season and an auspicious New Year to come!

The weather in this small Himalayan kingdom of Nepal is crisp and icy in the early mornings. Sparkling snow peaks rim the valley. The cold invigorates.

Keith sends his greetings from India where he moved after my visa trouble forced me to leave Darjeeling. He works on a translation of a Tibetan text about pilgrimage locations in Kathmandu, a manuscript I received as a gift from a Bhutanese man when I was on pilgrimage in Bodh Gaya last year. I gave it to Keith to translate. When he publishes it, he'll credit me with acquiring the unusual manuscript. I have a small collection of Tibetan manuscripts that would be nice to read and study someday.

Keith and I lived and traveled together for five years but in the last year we drifted apart. When we first lived in Darjeeling we shared a house, Angus Lodge, with Kanjur Rimpoche, Padma Wangyal's father. Recently Keith delved more deeply into his Tibetan work and I focused on mandala research and painting. Our separation enables both of us to pursue our individual interests.

Keith received a lot of praise for his first published book of Tibetan prayers he collected and translated with the help of Padma Wangyal. The title is *Ornaments of Illumination: The Sacred Path of Omniscience.* It was printed by G. Tharchin at the Tibet Mirror Press, Kalimpong. We still have very strong connections, but our karma draws us in different directions. If he continues to translate Tibetan manuscripts he will no doubt do great work.

Again, many thanks for all the little remembrances of cards, letters and packages. Truly enjoy an auspicious New Year.

Kathmandu
January 1971

This year promises surprise and excitement. May 1971 be more inspirational and rewarding than last year!

Next month I'll begin teaching English at the U.S.I.S. just after the Tibetan New Year, or *Losar.* The Tibetan New Year will be a climax especially for William, who I mentioned in my last letter. His work over the last three years will culminate in a seven-day Tibetan ceremony where the monks propitiate the deity Mahakala, the central figure of William's dissertation research. I've arranged to film part of the ceremony. A musicologist colleague, Terry Beck, will tape the soundtrack of the seven-day ritual.

Late spring might be the right time to return to the west. The possibility excites me. I am not alone in my plan to return. William will also return in March or April. William proves to be a great friend and companion. We both have the same lama, Sabchu Tulku, as a teacher.

Keith is well in India, but he seems very far away. Kathmandu, a large city in an isolated valley, bristles with energy: many Americans, Tibetans, Nepalese, Chinese, and even Russians live here. An international array of goods from India, Japan, China, and Russia are sold in the marketplace.

Although India is a much larger country, the Himalayas divide Nepal into many isolated valleys and areas where different languages are spoken. A journey from one isolated part of Nepal to another may take days or weeks on foot. Nepal is amazingly self-sufficient for such an isolated small inland country. Travel within the valley is quick and easy to arrange by private taxi or public bus.

William & me

c/o US Embassy
Kathmandu
Late January 1971

A geodesic dome might be a good solution for housing on the ranch. It can easily be assembled, moved, and reassembled. A yurt might be an interesting option to explore, too. Tibetan and Mongolian nomads live in round tents called yurts which are also portable and allow easy shelter for nomad yak herders who constantly move their animals to new grazing spots. The yurts are made from animal skins or thick woolen yak blankets.

I agreed to type a draft of William's Mahakala dissertation for Columbia University's Department of Near and Far Eastern Studies. I will transliterate the text for him as I type. That is, since I can read the Tibetan script, I can transpose the Tibetan letters to their English equivalents. There is no typewriter that has Tibetan script, so this is the only way to transcribe the text.

Please write soon and tell me what day of the week I was born on. This is very important.

How special to celebrate your thirty-sixth wedding anniversary! Congratulations to you and Dad! Did I mention the four stages of life according to Hindu philosophy? They are childhood, student, householder, and finally the ascetic lifestyle in old age where one renounces family life.

Of course, this is a gross simplification, but more and more I am considering my role in this time and place. No matter what, I'll be a perpetual student since learning is a lifelong process. I turn twenty-five this year. If I live to reach a hundred, this year marks a quarter of my life that has passed. Perhaps the time to generate family roots and settle into the house holding stage has come. What do you think?

Keltole

Kathmnadu

Late, late January 1971

To start I send all good wishes for today and for every consecutive day that we have the good fortune to witness the beauty of life. Sorrow is a perception we must work to exclude from our minds. We're human. Humans err and suffer—this is a reality. But it is also possible to be happy and content which I certainly hope you are.

Sometimes I think I dwell too much in my thoughts. I'm preoccupied with philosophical questions and answers. Hopefully I can use this penchant for meditation in a creative way. To let go of the snags and obstacles associated with greed, laziness, and lust is a continual challenge. But really, I'm very happy here now. I don't mean to give you a different impression by my philosophizing!

This new year is very significant for me. Probably by next year I can see just how significant it was...but for now I can only feel the intensity of each passing moment. We recently had a large tea party to celebrate William's birthday. Many friends came including Tibetan scholars from England and France. Johan Reinhard, an adventurer, mountain climber and high-altitude archeologist who is moving to Peru, told stories of a tribal encounter in the *terrai* region.

As you can see I acquired a typewriter. I'm about to begin the very big job of typing the dissertation that William is working on. As I mentioned before, we share a lot, most of what might be called attitude or purpose. There is a considerable difference between a westerner's and an easterner's attitude toward life. After living in the east for some time, I feel closer to the eastern traditions.

In the west, there is an emphasis on the development, nourish-ment, and extension of the ego. The eastern attitude, on the other hand, is to internalize the concept of self. That is, the idea of self and self-aggrandizement is minimalized. One strives to recognize self in relation to the entire cosmos. People prefer to flow easily within their natural surroundings and within their relationships and communi-ties. Flow rather than conquer, divide, subjugate. As a woman the concept of flow seems natural.

I am happy working on a small sutra about one of the Buddha's paradises. By "working," I mean I translate and visualize the images and ideas. The text elucidates my awareness of visualization. By thinking positive, healing thoughts, I hope to generate more positive thoughts. Good actions follow good thoughts. This is a simplified description of two steps on the eightfold path to achieve an enlight-ened mind.

Soon I will start teaching English to Nepalese students.

Our wedding

Kathmandu
Nepal
February 4, 1971

Are any of the flowers in the garden blooming yet? Here we celebrated the first day of Spring already.

I want to tell you of an important event. Undoubtedly, this will seem a surprise and a rapid development but actually the pace of life is quicker than what can be related in letters which take as long as two weeks in transit. My relationship with William may seem like a short one but I've actually known him for over a year. We met in Sarnath.

Well, we have decided to get married. We've discussed the idea and our decision is certain. He will arrange for his teacher, Manavajra Vajracarya, the priest of a large, local Newari temple, to marry us. The priest will perform the ceremony according to an ancient Buddhist tradition that was practiced during the 7th century in India and is still preserved in the rituals of the Newari or Nepali Buddhists.

Since the advent of Spring is a very good time in Kathmandu, our wedding will coincide with an auspicious arrangement of the stars. We will wed in a pine forest that was once sacred to the saint Nagarjuna. He blessed the site with his meditations many centuries ago.

Things happen so quickly. Now it will be impossible for you to come. In spite of the great distance, I will think of you all on that day as if you were here with us. Considering the six or more years that have already passed since we had the opportunity to see each other, I look forward to seeing you and introducing William to you as soon as we return.

Needless to say, I am excited! Although the decision to get married didn't seem so radical, the consequences are great and the significance even greater. I am thinking of you and everyone with love and confidence. I hope you can share in my joy.

Kathmandu

Nepal

February 1971

By now you have received my last letter, which must have been somewhat of a surprise! As I mentioned we decided to get married in a Nepalese Buddhist traditional ceremony and indeed, that is what we did, as you can see from the pictures enclosed. It was a fascinating ritual, full of symbolism which was significant for us because that is what we have been studying. It was a unique outdoor ceremony, probably never performed for westerners before. Since the priest was William's teacher and a very close friend for three years, it was very significant for him, too. I can't over-emphasize the culmination of karma which brought us together.

The occasion—the first day of spring—was very auspicious for the marriage.

According to legend, it is also the day when Lord Manjusri cut open the valley of Kathmandu with one swift stroke of his sword. He drained the lake and the land was opened for cultivation and habitation. I visited the place where the Bagmati river exits the valley; the gorge is very narrow and sharp just like the gorge in the myth.

The day was sunny and clear. After the outdoor ceremony in the Queen's forest outside Kathmandu, we feasted in the traditional fashion with no less than eighty-four carefully prepared dishes, symbolic of the marks of perfection on the body of a Buddha. The Newari repast prepared by Mana's wife and friends was amazing. Many dishes were completely new to us. Some were purely symbolic and were not really eaten (such as elephant meat!) We invited a small group of six friends to attend.

This must sound very strange and foreign to you. I have trouble myself following every aspect of the ritual even though I'm familiar with Buddhist ceremony. The ritual, which couldn't have been more beautiful, was a culmination of karma, like a well-deserved reward.

Although the specific aspects of Buddhist ritual are especially meaningful to me, I believe that any form or style or ritual or ceremony in other religions is just as significant to whoever participates in them. Ritual is a highly creative art: the offerings, the invocation of the central deity, which was Mahakala, the customs...even the location, a lovely pine forest all added to the beauty.

Well, dear Mother and Father, I hope you can understand a little of how I am feeling. I really hope you can share in some of my joy and excitement. The Tibetan Losar is coming up and I'm still planning to film some of the celebrations. The rinpoche of the monastery will perform a ceremony for an auspicious married life. This is really an exciting time. I would love to hear from you. Tell me all that you feel. I hope everyone is in excellent health and that happiness is plentiful and permanent.

P.S. William sends his deepest regards. He looks forward to meeting you soon.

Kathmandu

Nepal

February 23

Thank you so much for the two telegrams I received yesterday. I was so happy to hear from you so quickly. I'm very busy with teaching at the USIS. The local Nepalese students are shy and very polite. They have difficulty speaking up, but they enjoy reading and listening. I'm also working on the film I mentioned to document the Tibetan New Year ceremony which is coming soon. William is making copious notes as last minute references for his thesis.

The monks will construct a seven-foot-high image of the protecting deity, Mahakala. For seven continuous days they'll make offerings. The final day they carry all the decorative images and ritual *torma* cakes out to an open field and set them afire to burn away the year's old karma.

The film should be interesting, but we won't be able to see the results until we're back in the states where the film will be developed. I'm working with an ancient movie camera and the entire process is somewhat of a blind operation so we all have our fingers crossed.

Time really slips by. Spring must be beautiful in California. Here it is lovely, too. A visiting lama invited us to the mountains in Nepal where he lives with many Tibetan refugees. We could ride horses, climb mountains and experience life in the high elevations over 10,000 feet above sea level before we return to the west.

First, we need to finish our work here. Thank you again for the lovely telegrams. They really were sweet and I'm so glad you're pleased.

Manavajra prepares the homa puja fire.

Kathmandu
Monday
March 15, 1971

Two days ago, I went on a ride to the Chinese border where there is a hot spring. I enjoyed a hot bath but unfortunately my purse was stolen. Luckily my passport expires this month, so the possibility of misuse is slight. It is still difficult to get a new passport without the old one. This is the first time I lost my purse. William says it happens to everyone at least once. So considering that, I guess I'm lucky.

The USIS school shows movies every Friday as part of their program. Otherwise there are no English movies shown at the local theaters.

Kathmandu
March 17, 1971

Both William and I think that printing a notice in the *Palo Alto Times* is a good idea. This would let my Paly friends learn about my marriage. Just a short announcement like "On the first day of Spring, Jan. 31st in Kathmandu, Nepal, according to the Nepalese Buddhist tradition, William Byron George Stablein took Marilyn Estelle Zulch for his bride. The Ceremony was performed according to the traditional Buddhist Customs of Nepal."

We don't need a lot of publicity. A brief announcement is fine. You can add anything you deem pertinent, within reason of course. I'll send some photos. A simple photo of the outdoor ceremony in the Queen's Forest would be fine.

One reason you shouldn't publish all the details is that there is a legal complication which William is very apologetic for.

Now something about William: When he came to India four years ago he had a wife who more or less left him while he was waiting for a plane to India at the London Airport.

Although she later came to Nepal, they acknowledged that their personalities were organically opposite, and they agreed to go their respective paths. William heard that it was impossible to get a divorce in Kathmandu, so he didn't try to take any legal action. Meanwhile in the past weeks he has written some letters inquiring how to do this while living abroad.

Hence concerning American law, our marriage will not be considered absolutely legal until the complications are attended to on our return. This should be an easy formality. William is quite embarrassed by all of this but we both feel you should know. Here in Kathmandu it doesn't hinder our lives in any way, but we are concerned with the "proper way of being" as William puts it.

More about William: His father is a retired Presbyterian clergyman who was educated at the San Anselmo Theological Seminary in Marin County. His mother is apparently very dedicated to her family. He has one sister, older, who lives in Mahopac, New York, with her husband, a mathematician for IBM. She and her husband are classical pianists. William's parents for now look in a slightly askance manner on our romance as they are very much Old-Testament-oriented so it is difficult for them to wholeheartedly accept our marriage (under the aforementioned conditions).

At any rate, William loves his parents and is doing his best to work it out. He assures me they will be gently swayed. I didn't think it necessary to bring this up before as, frankly, it really has no bearing on our "true feelings."

It might take a while to legitimatize the marriage. I hope you can understand this. Although I know as a lawyer you are familiar with the ins and outs of the law, I also know you are a woman of the heart. I think I can assume that you will understand this temporary situation.

I'm reading Matsuo Basho's, *The Narrow Road to the Deep North.* The 17th century Buddhist poet left home early at the age of twenty-two and traveled on foot for five months to a northern province. His journal, written in the form of a *haibun,* a spiritual travel log interspersed with pithy, poetic haiku, captures the essence of his road travels. I admire his vision. He captures daily life in haiku-like moments of fresh insight. I left home three years earlier at nineteen and after five years I still walk ancient travelers' footpaths and circle temple ruins in the spirit of those who walked before me on pilgrimage.

Kathmandu

Late March 1971

More background on William. Ethnology is William's academic field with an emphasis on Tibetan culture. He is presently writing a paper which he will submit to Columbia University where he is a Doctoral Candidate. He wants to finish the main part of his thesis before we leave Nepal. We both have open tickets to the U.S. and we are waiting for William to finish his work before we plan where we'll live in the States.

William may have to return to N.Y. in June. Tentatively we plan to visit Seattle and Palo Alto and then live in New York until he finishes his doctorate. William's main desire is to continue as a research scholar, but as he points out, one's life is not always dictated by one's desire. Other considerations like politics and economics can change plans.

Anyway, it is difficult to say more about our plans after N.Y. We are both flexible and he says that we should always consider all things. We'll send some pictures you can use for the newspaper if you want. What do you think? My last letter mentioned my stolen purse. I'm getting a new passport, but it takes a while.

My teaching at the USIS (United States Information Service) is going well. I enjoy a pleasant walk to work through the crowded alleys of Kathmandu. The hot summer weather is slowly creeping up.

Kathmandu Nepal
March 28, 1971

Disregard my last mention of the stolen purse. It was returned after I paid a reward of $17. The matter was handled by a local man who has connections with the black market. Luckily, he was able to convince the thief to return the purse for a small reward. At any rate, he is illiterate and wouldn't know how to utilize my ID.

I'm thinking about insurance as I look ahead to a long plane ride home. Planes are riskier than slow moving vehicles. A slower vehicle crash is not as potentially devastating as a plane falling from a great altitude and crashing. Don't you think? There haven't been any hijackings in Asia yet, which is one advantage in flying from Asia east to the west coast.

We just moved to a nicer house across the Bagmati river which runs through Kathmandu. We have the upstairs flat and a couple, Jacques and Liz Bessin, live downstairs. She just gave birth to a baby girl yesterday. They are so excited. The house is in a beautiful location in the country away from city noise. This is our last move. We'll stay here for 1 1/2 months until the hot season.

This morning I saw an eight-foot-long snake cross the path in front of me! Since many creatures live in these isolated fields I need to watch where I step.

Vijyeshvari District
Kathmandu

April 7, 1971

The apartment complex on the Bayshore highway 101 that you mentioned in your letter sounds risky especially since the tenants are shady, as you say. The former Petaluma chicken ranch, on the other hand, has good potential. Land in the country is perfect for a retreat. Can't wait to see the eucalyptus trees and rolling hills with grazing sheep.

I still have a few legal questions you might be able to answer. Can William file for divorce from abroad? Which state would be better? Which state, Washington or California, has the shortest wait? Since both parties agree to dissolve the marriage doesn't that make the process easier? Ironically his ex-wife lives in Nepal and is willing to sign any paperwork.

A friend's father who is a lawyer in S.F. simply annulled his son's former marriage. Is an annulment a possibility? William has been separated for the three years he has lived abroad...is that grounds for an annulment?

I hate to trouble you with all this, but if it's not too much trouble to look up or consult with someone else, it would certainly help us plan our next move.

By the way, what kind of legal cases are you working on these days? You seem busy and happy with the household and your different projects and organizations. It is always better to be active. I feel this way, too. There is never enough time to do the things, all the things, that one should, could, or would like to do.

A friend, Nik Douglas, just returned from the region of Dolpo near the Tibetan border where he spent a month researching Tibetan

Buddhist woodblock prints. He collected both Buddhist and Bonpo prints. Bonpo is an indigenous offshoot of Buddhism. He plans to publish the hundreds of examples of prints. He helped the monks print copies from their ancient hand-carved wooden blocks.

Other friends with Dolpo connections include Addison Smith who leads trekking expeditions to the region and Dolpo Wangyal who teaches me thangka painting.

Kathmandu
April 28, 1971

At work I heard about the two trunk telephone calls that came yesterday. I'm so sorry I missed you! I presume there's nothing serious to report or you would have sent a telegram. What a fun idea to talk from so far away!

Again, I'm sorry I wasn't here when you called. Please try again! I'm at the U.S.I.S. on Tuesday, Wednesday, Thursday or Friday when I work from 3:30-4:30 Nepali time. So 4:30 would be best or in the evening. Our landlord Dr. Tuladar has a phone. He's the Director of Tourism (tel.#12008). We're usually home in the evening from 6 pm. but we should set a date and time in advance.

William and I have been talking about the possibilities for the ranch. I'd love to plant some fruit trees and bamboo. What's the climate like there? How much rainfall? What type of soil? Sunny? A picture would be nice.

Manavajra Vajracharya is an herbalist and ayurvedic practitioner, in addition to being a Newari priest, artist, and scholar. With him I study medicinal herbs for practical uses. William plans to do an extensive study of medicinal Himalayan plants if he receives a grant for the work. I could get seeds here to bring back. Maybe shoots or seedlings too but what kind I'm not sure. A natural fence of century plants would be practical.

There are many exciting possibilities. Don't rent out the old ranch house. It might be a good place for us while we get resettled. I look forward to seeing the land. It sounds great.

Bamboo, besides being a beautiful plant, is extremely hearty. The underground shoots are edible. Tropical fruit like mangoes or papayas would be nice to grow if there's enough sun.

Kathmandu
Nepal
May 29, 1971

Today is the last school day for the spring session. I have ten days off before the second term starts. The situation in East Pakistan is appalling. What's worse, there seems to be no end to it!

Our travel plans have shifted. There are a lot of projects here. We want to organize an exhibition and art sale to benefit the Tibetan Swayambhunath community. William set up a free clinic at the monastery. Dr. Bethyl Fleming, a Methodist missionary doctor, distributes medicines there once a week.

Every week more patients show up. The supply of medicine is almost depleted. We'd like to raise money to continue the clinic. The refugees from Tibet desperately need medical attention. Their physical condition is sad. They were so healthy in the higher altitudes of Tibet.

I type up parts of William's dissertation as he finishes them. He started publishing articles in academic journals. An article on Tantra & Yoga will be published in India and another paper for a Thai publication. He'd like to write a book but needs to complete his doctorate first.

Please bear with us as we extend our departure date until July or August. It's best to finish as many projects as we can before we leave.

Any suggestions for raising a little money for the monks' medicine would be appreciated. An organization which could recognize tax deductible donations is hard to set up here. Maybe Dad has information on charitable donations? Just an idea.

After my last English classes are over today, the teachers are invited to the Director Bob Cutler's house for a Nepali lunch of okra and tomato curry, lentil soup, whole wheat flat bread, dahi (yogurt), an array of chutneys, probably tamarind, lemon and parsley, and milk rice pudding.

Kathmandu

June 23, 1971

The monsoon season is on time and it rains every afternoon. Most of the days are sunny. Sometimes a gentle night rain falls.
Fruit stalls in the local market overflow with mangoes and branches of freshly picked lychees still covered with the papery sacks to peel off. Inside, the glistening pearly white fruits.

There is something concerning us these days. Something more than the weather and external physical activities. If the prospect of becoming grandparents is just a portion of the excitement of becoming parents, then I think you know how we feel. As you can see, what I'm hinting at is I'm expecting a baby in October.

We're both excited about this and now there is even more to look forward to. We waited to tell you but now the risky period is over. I'm healthy and happy. The baby is due in mid-October. My pregnancy doesn't affect our overall plan to return except that we need to consider the best time to travel after we complete our work here. And the difficulty of undertaking a long journey in the seventh or eighth month.

Marriage in January and first born in October was also your experience, wasn't it? Was Alice's birth the same year, too?

William wrote his parents about the news, but we haven't heard from his mother yet. We sincerely hope that they can put aside their "Old Testament" concerns and share our excitement with us.

My health is great. There have been no complications. Dr. Bethyl Fleming, the missionary doctor who fifteen years ago founded the Shanta Bhavan, the best hospital in Nepal, will be my gynecologist. You can read about her and her husband in *The Fabulous Flemings of Kathmandu*. She reminds me of Nanny with her long white braid and benign, grandmotherly nature. She is very congenial and although she is retired she is full of inexhaustible energy. Her husband is an ornithologist who discovered a few rare species of Himalayan birds.

William's work is coming along. I just finished typing the Sanskrit text so there are a few more odds and ends to finish before he can send it to his professor. He and his Newari informant and teacher, Dr. Manavajra Vajracharya—we call him Mana—plan to write a book illustrated with Mana's illustrations of Newari ritual. He is also the priest who married us.

Kathmandu

July 18, 1971

I purchased some fabrics in the cloth market to make a quilt for the baby. I never learned how to quilt but I think I can improvise hand stitching squares onto a background fabric, probably soft flannel. A friend has a hand-powered antique sewing machine but it's easier to stitch by hand.

Calcium tablets are available in the drugstore, but I wonder what strength is good? Multi-vitamins also have calcium. Mana jokingly recommends a Newari tonic made from pulverized water buffalo bones which are naturally rich in calcium. I tried some of the powder in a cup of chai. Not a bad idea or concoction. I've been a little sick with a monsoon virus the last week: fever, cough, cold, headache. But with rest and some prescribed medicine I feel a lot better.

The monsoon season is an unhealthy one in the Kathmandu Valley. Hepatitis, flu and dysentery are very prevalent. We manage OK because I boil our water for twenty five minutes, filter it with a sand filter from the Peace Corps organization, and then boil the water again! Also, a gamma globulin shot protects me from getting hepatitis.

I'm still teaching elementary English at the USIS. Our art exhibition will begin next week. We hope to sell sketches of Nepalese community life to benefit the medical clinic for the monks I wrote about.

Some interesting news for me anyway is that my teacher in Sonada last year, Kalu Rinpoche, has gone to Canada! This hasn't been absolutely confirmed but most reports hint at such a move. The Canadian government set up a small Tibetan refugee relocation settlement in British Columbia, which as you know isn't that far from California.

William keeps pretty busy and I help where I can. Eventually things will resolve and we will return. We'd really like to see the monastery fitted out with running water and some decent latrines, but carpentry, plumbing skills, and supplies are hard to come by here.

Kathmandu

August 1, 1971

Ironically after all the questions I asked about the possibility of getting a divorce abroad, a divorce was granted to William last week in the Nepali court! It was a very tiring one day affair with lots of paper work. Nepalese legal documents, interestingly enough, are handwritten in a Nepalese cursive script with old fashion pens dipped into ink. The text is written on handmade rice paper and stitched together with needle and thread! No staplers in Nepal I guess. It's a curio for sure.

Also, the divorce is rumored to be the first divorce granted in Nepal and was only possible since both the ex-wife and William were present and stated they had no objections. We probably saved a lot of money by going to court here. The American embassy assured us they will recognize the Nepalese court verdict...so all is well in that area, which is a relief.

We're now planning to have the baby be born here in Kathmandu since we are comfortable and relatively at home here. I'm hoping we can all get together with family (after seven years for me!) for Christmas. I plan to rest and not travel until six or eight weeks after the birth.

A Nepalese cook named Dede comes a few days a week. This seems the most sensible plan. William is busy as ever and can use the extension of time to finish up. I'm working with a group of friends to publish a collection of our poems. Although we're disappointed to have to put off our return some more, we will be completing some good work here.

A young American, a Theravadin monk in Thailand for three years, is funding the Tibetan monastery renovation. His strong discipline and religious commitment to help the monks is heart-warming. The monks are very excited about the latrine, kitchen remodel, and other practical and cosmetic upgrades (paint, exterior stucco). Improvements in their daily life, they believe, will also help them in their religious work. We agree and are very happy we could help make the renovations possible.

Thankfully the difficult monsoon season doesn't dampen spirits here but seems to stimulate action and progress in many areas.

Kathmandu

August 17, 1971

After I teach today I visit a physiotherapist to learn exercises to help facilitate a natural birth. William taught me the basic Tai Chi Chuan exercises he learned in New York with Da Liu, a Chinese instructor. The exercises, centered in the abdomen or chi, are also a good way to prepare for childbirth.

My weight is up from a hundred and twenty-five pounds. Last week I weighed in at one hundred fifty-five—30 pounds over! With two more months I can't imagine carrying around any more weight.

This is an active month. For a local Nepalese celebration called Gunla, musicians visit many holy sites in the valley. They play as they walk to the Svayambhunath temple from across the river. I can hear their bands every morning at 3:30 a.m.

William works on both his book with Mana about Nepalese religious ceremony and also on his dissertation on Mahakala. Every day I type a few pages for him which I enjoy. The subject matter is interesting.

I photographed a number of the unusual architectural styles of the stupa reliquaries that are so abundant in every courtyard or temple compound. Some have the usual symbolic shapes: square (earth), circle (water), half moon, flame on top. Others have multiple tiers and sometimes even little niches that can house tiny Buddha statues. It would be nice to one day publish a series of photographs I took in Nepal to accompany poems.

The benefit exhibition opens this month at a local gallery. Paul Grover, a painter friend, will show paintings of the monks and lamas engaged in their daily work at the monastery. We hope to raise some money for the medical clinic. I'll let you know about the opening on the 27th.

Since I'm interested in Tibetan astrology, one of the monks I work with gave me a Tibetan manuscript on a few aspects of the Tibetan traditional astrological studies. It is a large loose-leaf manuscript, unbound, measuring two feet across and ten inches wide and tall. Two people are needed to lift it. I enjoy looking through it but need

to learn another (more complicated) script in order to figure out what it says. That's one of my next projects. At least if I copy the text in the more familiar *dbu chen* script it will be easier to read in the future.

Mom, with your experience of having six kids, do you have any notion or possible clues to learning the baby's sex? Just curious. It's raining heavily and quite cool, but the next two months are some of the loveliest weather-wise.

Kathmandu

Nepal

August 22, 1971

As far as we can tell the baby is due in about six weeks. The Nepalese woman who helps cook agreed to come every day after the birth so I can relax at home for six weeks and not worry about shopping and cooking. The market is a half mile walk from home and without refrigeration we need to buy fresh food daily to prevent spoilage. The Nepalese recommend keeping a newborn indoors at home for six weeks as a precaution.

Our plan is still to return in December. Xmas would be a nice date to aim for. William may take a short job photocopying some Sanskrit and Tibetan manuscripts for a library in Stony Brook, New York, the Institute for Advanced Studies in World Religions.

William and I both look forward to seeing the ranch in Petaluma. We like your idea about setting up some sort of retreat. A permanent library for books, a herbal botanical garden with Himalayan herbs and plants, and renovations to the old farmhouse would be nice. Winter in Bodega Bay would be warmer than Seattle, where William's parents live, or Vancouver, BC where a Kargyupa Tibetan center is under construction.

The west holds great possibilities and the ranch is really ideal. If we had the means, we'd bring a selection of our Tibetan monk friends with us. We would all be very happy in a nice country setting.

We'll legalize our marital status this week which means a name change for me.

Today is a beautiful day to celebrate my birthday. I'm enjoying everything immensely. Thank you for your card and good wishes.

Kathmandu

Nepal

August 25, 1971

The exhibit opened with a nice reception. This happens to be a vacation time for most of the Americans working here so we haven't sold as many paintings as expected. But we're happy with any amount since it benefits the monastery.

Last Thursday, after the head abbot selected an auspicious day, he proclaimed us officially married after a short ceremony on the roof of the Svayambhunath gompa which was attended by an official from the embassy to document and legalize the necessary paperwork.

It was a lovely sunny morning. All our lama friends lined up and took turns presenting each of us with a white scarf ceremonially placed around our necks, a Tibetan custom. For the rickshaw ride home, we bundled together dozens of white scarves. It was one of the clearest mornings of the monsoon. A beautiful rainbow circled the sun which Pecham claimed was an auspicious omen that predicted a happy marriage.

The next six weeks will be exciting. My neighbor downstairs who has a five- month-old daughter, recommended a few necessities. Would you, Mom, be willing to ship a few clothes for the baby? That would be wonderful. Baby oil, powder, soap and paper diapers I can get from the commissary through a friend. My cook will wash cloth diapers, no problem. But a pair of rubber baby pants, a nursing bra (size? maybe 36 B), and a few baby clothes that are not available here would be so great. If you label any package a Gift Parcel no duty is charged.

I hope this is not too much trouble. I think it is best to have everything ready at home before coming back from the hospital. Maybe you could stick in a pair of panties or if you think of anything else.

Kathmandu

August 31, 1971

Today is rather cool and the overcast rather damp here. We're looking forward to October with the clear blue skies and the snowy peaks visible again. Liz's mother visited for a month. She enjoyed meeting her granddaughter, visiting with Liz and Jacques and seeing Nepal. She hand-carried part of William's dissertation to Columbia University to give to his professor. He's still working on the Index and Appendix which I can type before the baby comes.

We enjoyed visiting with Liz's mother so much we're wondering if you and Bill feel adventurous and would like to visit us in Kathmandu! We're sure you'd enjoy the change. You could experience an eastern culture. We'll make sure you'll be comfortable. Maybe stay with us. But if the quarters are too small here there are nice places in town. After the air fare expense living here is relatively inexpensive.

We'd love to see you and show you around. You could meet the baby. November is a beautiful month and I'd be a little more mobile with the baby. You could meet our Tibetan friends at the monastery. Bill would enjoy the trip. Anyway, it's an idea.

I discontinued teaching since I don't want to get overworked by the walk into town and back four days a week. I'm in good health but a shrimp dinner didn't agree with me last night. We still plan on returning in mid-December.

Kathmandu
September 17, 1971

You don't need to worry about the local drinking water. The restaurants boil their drinking water. I boil our water for twenty minutes and then filter it also. After the monsoon season ends, in October or November, is a healthier time to visit.

About our N.Y plans. William must go to NYC to defend his dissertation and finish a required French language course. We're open to any job offers he may get. His dissertation is interesting to read as I type it.

Stanford has a Far Eastern Studies Department. I wonder if they offer Tibetan or Sanskrit courses? It would be convenient to relocate to the west coast.

Kathmandu
September 24, 1971

Dr. Fleming thinks the baby won't arrive for another three weeks. So, I have time to prepare. I ordered a basket woven out of cane and bamboo from the local cottage industry Craft Coop. They are customarily slow, but they promised to have it finished this week. I designed it like a bassinette. Aren't bassinettes made of bamboo? Mine won't have legs but I'll swing it from the ceiling. It will also have a large handle, so we can pick the basket up like an Easter basket and easily transport the baby.

I also ordered a large hand-bound book made with paper from a local factory or workshop studio. The beige paper, like rice paper, has a very organic feel which I like. I can collage the pages when I get back with papers from my ephemera collection. One curio is a vintage Buddhist tourist pamphlet from the 1930s to entice pilgrims from Burma to visit Bodh Gaya, the central pilgrimage site and center of the Buddhist world.

William may apply to the Institute of Mental Health for a grant to study the use of ayurvedic medicine in the religious ceremonies of Nepal. He would research how the medicines are associated with mental health. He wishes he had a library of Medical Anthropology books to consult as he drafts his proposal.

Kathmandu

October 25, 1971

I expect you received the telegram William sent to announce the birth on October 15 at 8:50 a.m. A nice big baby boy weighed in at eight pounds and fourteen ounces. I relaxed a week in the hospital. There is no rush to send the mother home here. I felt like I was in a resort. My window had a lovely view of the snow-capped peaks. The baby sleeps in a small crib next to my bed. He has a touch of jaundice which should disappear soon, I'm told.

I enjoy the Nepalese style of life after childbirth. Every day I have a hot oil bath and massage in the hot sun. As soon as the baby is over the jaundice he'll join me. Our cook is also a masseuse. She washes diapers every day by hand.

William accepted a job to microfilm some ancient Sanskrit and Tibetan manuscripts, so we need to delay our departure until after Christmas. While I was pregnant it was hard to imagine having another person join our household. The baby is very alert and happy. We have a lot of fun just watching him in his world. I'll send a picture soon.

We're thinking of naming him after William. We both like the idea. For now, we mostly call him Pugu (Tibetan for baby).
I must close since it's feeding time. Stay well and happy.

Kathmandu

November 1, 1971

I was quite exhausted the first week home from the hospital, so I apologize for not writing sooner. Thank you for your telegram. The

William & Willie

baby sleeps and eats more regularly now. We're getting used to his needs and schedule. His jaundice is clearing up.

We did decide to name him William Jr.

The doctor recommended a BCG injection for T.B. which is prevalent here. The only concern is that in the future the usual patch test done back home will appear positive, so it will be hard to detect if he does become infected with tuberculosis.

Our cook keeps busy shopping, washing and cooking. She is a real boon.

William's sister has a son, so this is the second grandson for his parents.

Kathmandu

November 29, 1971

Baby Willie is growing quickly and has a sweet smile. Our plan is to
return in April, so if you would like to visit before then that would be
nice. Bill would love the mountains. This is the best season to visit:
clear skies and snowy peaks all day long!

We'd love to see you and you can meet the baby.

For Thanksgiving dinner, William organized a party with ten
stuffed ducks deliciously catered by a local restaurant.

Now that the baby is six-weeks-old, we will start to take him on
outings. First to the monastery and a picnic this Thursday. His health
is excellent. I've had some bothersome boils on my leg and a sty in
my eye but both are clearing up. My energy level is low.

Yes, the baby was born in the hospital established by Dr. Fleming.
I am Rh negative and William positive so perhaps that's why the
jaundice? Even the Tibetan horoscope chart predicted the baby
would have trouble with bile. He is well now.

Kathmandu

December 7, 1971

I'm curious how long this letter takes to reach you. The Indian-
Pakistan war disrupts mail and banking. We're fine in spite of the
mail and travel delays. Even though we're a lot closer to the fighting
we don't receive any communication except infrequent English radio
news. You probably have the current news.

I was surprised when I weighed Willie Jr. yesterday. At seven
weeks he weighs fourteen pounds and more. He certainly prospers.
More color photos coming.

On the day of the last Full Moon, the Rinpoche at the monastery
gave him a Tibetan name: Tsering Dondup, meaning "he whose life
will be long and full of meaningful accomplishments." Mana gave
him a Nepalese name, Meghavahin, "he who rides the clouds." And

with his middle name Paul, he has three respective societies and traditions to look up to.

We chose Paul because of Dad, grandpa Paul. William's mother likes Paul since it reminds her of St. Paul and as she said, the last syllable of the country of Ne-pal is pronounced Paul.

I'm taking penicillin to treat the boils and the sty. The doctor says my resistance is low after giving birth but otherwise I feel good and managed to strap Willie on my back to walk into town last week. There are no baby carriages here. Even if there were strollers can't maneuver over the ancient cobblestone alleys.

When we visited Dr. Fleming she gave us a small blanket for Willie. She is really nice and reminds me so much of Nanny, especially with the long white braid.

Kathmandu

December 24, 1971

With great excitement we received your letter and the news of your visit! The mail has been delayed so I didn't write before this. Sorry if it's been a long time. At least the war is over and as far as I can see communication and travel are restored.

So January 10! We're anxious to see you and my dear older brother, Bill! Let us know the exact details. Do you arrive here January 10? Are hotels and meals included in your travel package? How long is your trip? Sorry for so many questions.

We can plan accordingly. You'll love Kathmandu. Maybe we could travel to Sarnath together.

The Director of the USIS, Tom Dove, invited us to Christmas dinner so I hope we can meet the proper protocol with baby Willie. I would never leave him alone with a babysitter. Wherever I go, he comes too. Let's hope he's on his best behavior tonight. He really doesn't cry much and smiles a lot.

All our best wishes for a wonderful Christmas.

Kathmandu

December 26

Today is the 26th. Christmas dinner was a banquet! The food was delicious and the company fascinating. I designed a velvet jumper worn with a long silk blouse. The jumper's embroidered straps unsnapped so I could discretely breastfeed in a corner. But once the baby woke up and ate, he was thrilled with all the softly colored lights, polished furnishings, the murmur of people talking, laughing, and the sound of glasses tinkling. He stayed awake the rest of the evening.

Kathmandu

December 29

The New Year is almost here. May the whole family have an auspicious and prosperous year ahead! I look forward to welcoming you to Nepal.

We had a cold spell—it is the Himalayas—so I need to remind you to bring plenty of warm clothes just in case. India is not so cold.

We're used to the cold and don't have any kind of heating, so you may find our home on the chilly side.

Willie doesn't like artificial heat. One night we took him out to eat and he hated the stuffy overheated dining room. He cried until I took him outside.

The first day home from the hospital, I bundled him up snuggly thinking he had a fever. At home he howled in protest. We were completely baffled. I finally took some of his clothes off and he quieted right down. So now I don't worry about him getting too cold. I just imagined the fever.

We are anxiously awaiting your arrival. When can we expect you?

Dr. Fleming gave Willie some scented baby oil, body lotion, and a soft pillow. He loved the lights on her Christmas tree. She is very thoughtful and kind.

Before the birth I completed the handstitched yellow and black patchwork baby quilt. The yellow patches are calico designs. I stitched a green tie dye trim around the quilt for the border. The backside is soft flannel. I studied how to quilt. I experimented by stitching the patches directly onto the flannel backing. It works fine.

My mother & brother

Kathmandu
February 18, 1972

What a great visit we had together in Kathmandu. A very memorable occasion after seven years! Thanks for making the long trip. I look forward to your photos.

We were glad to hear everything went smoothly on your return trip. After you left we had a cold spell which left traces of snow on the peaks surrounding the valley. It rained and was very cold. Glad you brought the sunshine with you.

Our Tibetan and Nepalese friends enjoyed meeting you. We hope Bill enjoyed the trip. We thought of him on the 15th, his birthday, which was celebrated here as the Tibetan New Year.

William is planning a trip to India to microfilm Tibetan manuscripts for the Institute for Advanced Studies on World Religions Library in Stony Brook, N.Y. We might all take a quick trip to India for two weeks.

Willie Jr. is already 15 lbs! Somehow the baby scales were mixed up earlier. He stayed healthy even when we both had colds.

William and his musicologist friend Terry Beck taped the seven-day ceremony of the Mahakala Puja at the monastery which occurs every New Year. For the professional recording they borrowed hi-fidelity equipment from the USIS valued at over $50,000. We're exploring how to publish the educational recording of indigenous Tibetan ritual folk music.

The stamps on the outside envelope portray the Hindu version of Mahakala.

In planning for our return I'll send my collection of 150 Tibetan woodblock prints printed on Nepalese handmade paper. Please acknowledge when the air mail package arrives. Thanks in advance.

Kathmandu

March 3, 1972

Thanks for the French flash cards to help William study for his doctoral language requirements at Columbia University.
On the plane back we'll ship all the valuable thangkas, statues, paintings, yantras, and mandalas as air cargo. I don't want to ship irreplaceable texts and art by sea mail.

Yesterday I took our Tibetan manuscripts to the Museum of Archeology to get official approval to "export" our "historical" documents out of the country. The staff will affix "OK to Export" tags of "approval" for each item. The tags, sealed with red sealing wax, will be tied to each item. It's important to get the clearance before we travel. We don't want anything confiscated at the airport.

When I board the plane, my hands will be full carrying Willie Jr. and a few shoulder bags as carry-ons. I need to ship our libraries ahead of us. Published books like the Tibetan and Sanskrit dictionaries are theoretically replaceable so if something happens to them in route to California we can get replacements.

Kathmandu
March 18, 1972

The baby blue sweater and blanket for Willie arrived finally. The package was sent Sept. 26, 1971. All I can say is that I'm glad it arrived five months late instead of eight months because he would have completely outgrown the beautiful sweater. He looks adorable in it!

I started supplementing breast milk after five months. In the first two days he finished two jars of baby food from Aunt Jane—you met her when we ate buffalo burgers at her popular Aunt Jane's Restaurant. She bought the baby food and some disposable diapers at the commissary for me. I'll add egg yolks to the baby's diet next because I don't want to depend on processed canned food. Who knows what preservatives are put in baby foods. Fresh food is always the best.

We're toying with the idea of bringing Dolpo Wangyal to America. He could support himself painting and selling Tibetan thangkas. He's the artist who gave you the Long Life woodblock print. Before he arrives, he'll need proper immigration papers. We can be financial guarantees, but he'll need an employer to get a Green Card.

William hopes you can follow up and call his mother in Seattle and tell her about your visit with us. She worries a lot. It would reassure her to hear about your trip.

We still have a lot of loose ends to tie up in the next two months before we leave in early June. William may apply for a grant to finish his dissertation.

Kathmandu

April 4, 1972

Baby Willie has two teeth! When they came in he had a fever but luckily it vanished. He also sits up. He'll probably be crawling by the time we arrive. Good to leave behind the mud floor before the baby begins to crawl.

Last night we attended a dinner in honor of Dr. Stella Kramish, an expert on Nepalese Art who has worked in the field for at least 30 years. She is 76 years old. The ambassador was present as were many dignitaries. I kept the baby awake all day so he'd be sure to sleep soundly in an upstairs bedroom. So, what do you think happened? He stayed up until 11 pm, two hours later than usual. He enjoyed the excitement.

Kathmandu

May 2, 1972

What a nice surprise to talk over the phone! Even with the slight clicking noises of the long distant trunk call, it was amazing to hear your voice. I hardly knew what to say.

In the last month we enjoyed goodbye dinners with friends. We know a number of anthropologists specializing in Tibetan and Nepalese culture: Sandy MacDonald from Paris, Don Messerschmidt a former Peace Corps Volunteer who worked in Nepal a number of years, and Johan Reinhard who specializes in high altitude scuba diving expeditions. Joe is moving to Peru to study and research the Inca civilization in the Andes mountains.

As I mentally adjust to leaving our home after these years, so many friends and acquaintances spring to mind. A number of American and Canadian friends have taken the vows of monastic life like Dharmadipo the Theravadin monk from California, Sakya Dorje from Canada and Tsultrim Allione, a nun in the Tibetan tradition ordained by H.H. Karmapa. Tsultrim wore a large mala or Tibetan rosary around her neck as she picked up baby Willie and bounced him on her lap. As soon as he saw her beads he latched onto them and wouldn't let go. They fascinated him.

OK. Enough reminiscing! I need to get back to work.

If I don't get another chance to sit down and write a letter, I'll call in route. We'll stay overnight in Thailand and land in Seattle early June.

I'll share an odd, recurring dream: I return to Palo Alto. When I see you drive by in the old family station wagon, I'm so excited I shout from the sidewalk: "I'm back! Hello! I'm back!"

But you drive right by, not recognizing your own daughter.

I don't know what to expect as I return home. Of course, I'm not the single woman, teenage traveler I was when I left. I return with a husband, a child, and seven years worth of notebooks, manuscripts, paintings, and memories of living in the east. I hope to write about my travels one day.

Epilogue

The letters stop in early May 1972 as William and I made last minute preparations to return to the states with baby Willie and two foot-lockers full of Tibetan manuscripts, paintings, notebooks, and art. We also hand carried letters from Tibetan friends to mail for them in the States and wedged presents for our families into our luggage. William had been away for four years and was anxious to complete his Mahakala doctoral work at Columbia. Since I had been away almost twice that long, my transition from expat-cum-traveler to wife and mother took some adjustment. My studies were put on hold.

We landed in Seattle where William grew up. Immediately I felt at home in the University District's bookstores and art house movie theaters: Grand Illusion, Seven Gables and the University Theater. We discovered a coffee roasting start-up located at the very bottom level of the five story Public Market on the waterfront. No brewed coffee was available at the first retail shop—of the now ubiquitous Starbuck's chain of coffee houses—just burlap bags full of whole beans. The pungent aroma of freshly roasted coffee—like an exotic stimulating elixir—stirred long ago memories. Bookstores and coffee shops! Had I really been away seven years?

After a stop in Palo Alto to visit my family, we continued on to New York where we settled in the gatekeeper's cottage on the old Tinker Estate in the village of Poquott, on the eastern end of Long Island. The founder of the Institute for Advanced Studies of World Religions at the University of New York, at the Stony Brook Melville Library, hired William to translate the *Mahaparinirvana Sutra* from the Tibetan. He commuted into New York to finish his Columbia University doctoral requirements. Our daughter Sunita was born six months later. After William received his doctorate, we relocated to Seattle.

The South East Asia department at the University of Washington, Seattle, offered many classes relevant to India, Tibet, and Nepal stud-ies. When I enrolled at the Jackson School of International Studies in 1977 twelve years had passed between my freshman and sophomore college years. I was older than the other students but grateful that I had a focus that eluded me as a younger student. For a number of university papers I was able to utilize personal research, drawings, and notes on Tibetan arts and crafts.

Tibetologist Turrell Wylie, who developed the most frequently used system for transliterating the Tibetan language into roman letters, became a mentor. What is known as the Wylie transliteration, is used for transcribing Tibetan words in academic and historical contexts. Since I visited, on numerous occasions, many of the geographical locations of pilgrimage places in India and Nepal, I enjoyed studying Wylie's work *A Tibetan Religious Geography of Nepal* (Instituto Italiano per il Medio Ed Estremo Oriente, 1970).

I also worked with the Austrian born linguist, scholar, and anthropologist Agehananda Bharati who taught in the Southeast Asian department. A Sanskrit scholar and ordained Hindu monk, he lived in India for many years. As editor of the *Tibet Society Journal* in 1978 he published a paper I wrote based on my tantra notes, charts, maps, and observations living and traveling to Buddhist sacred sites: "Textual and Contextual Patterns of Tibetan Buddhist Pilgrimage in India."

I welcomed the opportunity to study pilgrimage in retrospect, from an anthropological, spiritual perspective. For the first time I could view and interpret aspects of my journey through an academic lens.

Around the same time, I began to hone my writing skills at various Creative Writing workshops in poetry at the University of Washington, and fiction and nonfiction workshops at the University of Houston. Essays I wrote in Philip Lopate's Creative Nonfiction class were later published in my memoir, *Sleeping in Caves: A Sixties Himalayan Memoir*. In fiction workshops Donald Barthelme guided me with his unique blend of postmodern sardonic witticisms, sensibilities, and aesthetics. A few of the stories I wrote then appeared in *The Census Taker: Tales of a Traveler in India and Nepal*.

In Seattle I also began to explore opportunities to use creative work in the context of performance art. Versions of *Himalayan Travelogs,* a piece I developed working with musicians, dancers, spoken word, chants, projected imagery, props, and art installations, was performed first at On the Boards performance space and later at the Intiman Theater during the annual Bumbershoot Festival.

Although the letters and handwritten aerograms which took weeks and sometimes months to arrive were not written with any thought of publication, they offer a glimpse into a distant time and place from a young American artist's perspective decades before the internet, texting and social media. The letters join an eclectic archive of 1960s travel ephemera, art, notes, maps, woodblock prints, poems, documents, objects and artifacts that still evoke and inspire new work: visual collage journals, artist books, writing and new projects.

Acknowledgements

A warm thank you and *namaste* to the host of travelers, scholars, saints, rinpoches, gurus, friends, expats, and associates I encountered—some however briefly—during my years in India and Nepal from 1966-1972. This incomplete list may reflect a sampling of Tibetan, Hindu, Burmese, Nepalese, Asian, American, British, and European friends, mentors, sponsors and hosts who contributed to a diverse multicultural and spiritual community.

Scholars, Travelers, Practitioners

Alex Wayman tibetologist
Johan Reinhard anthropologist
Alexander Berzin tibetan archivist
Dr. Bethel Fleming MD
Robert Fleming ornithologist
Don Messerschmidt anthropologist
William Stablein tibetologist
Christopher George tibetologist
Robert Thurman tibetologist
Robert Gross anthropologist
Rex Jones anthropologist
Shirley Kurz Jones anthropologist
Alexander MacDonald French anthropologist
Terry Beck musicologist
Cherie Bremer Kamp
Stella Kramrisch art historian
Mary Slusser art historian
E. Gene Smith Tibetan manuscript archivist
Anagarika Govinda German Buddhist scholar
Li Gotami painter, wife of Lama Govinda
Sunyabhai Alfred Sorensen, Danish hermit

Svetoslav Roerich son of Nicholas Roerich, Russian Peace Activist
Devika Rani film actress
Vito Victor
Steve and Ondine Shapiro
Peter Nawang Tendup Cooper
Lodro Thaye
Dharmadipo and Annapurna
Sonam Chutso and Sherab Tharchin
Joseph Goldstein
Jasper Ram Giri Newsome
Nico Morrison
Nik Douglas
Andy Klein
Sakya Dorje
John Myrdhin Reynolds
John Weir and Tsewang Hardy
Ken and Ingrid McLeod
Richard Tenzing Mueller
Terry Clifford
Arthur Mandelbaum
Turina
Maria Monroe
Maya Lama
Paul Gyss
Katarina Moraiti
Hartley and Ramona Appleton
Rick and Julie Flowerday
Keith and Chris Redman
Hannah and Lama Ole Nydhal
Richard Lama Padma and Susan Baldwin
Paul and Gina Tuell
Rick and Anne Kitaeff
Eight Finger Eddie
Tsultrim Allione
Sixter Max

Zena Rachevesky
Vimala Thakur Hindu mystic
Ram Dass (Richard Alpert)
Bhagavan Das
Terris and Sonja Temple
Hubert and Martisa Decleer
Bob and Shirley Cutler
Paul and Hope Grover
Keith Dowman
Steve Landsburg
Addison Smith
Michal Abrams
Jon and Lynn Weinberger
Jan and Nel Mascall
Stephanie Prince
Richard Volkman
Richard Horn
David Padwa
Harold Talbot
Roger and Gina Williams
Simon
Clive Giboire
Bonnie Corbin

Tibetans

H.H. the Dalai Lama, Dharamsala
Chatral Sangye Dorje Rinpoche, Ghoom
Tarthang Tulku, Varanasi
H.H. Dudjom Rinpoche, Darjeeling
H.H. Drukpa Thuksey Rinpoche
Thinley Norbu Rinpoche
Kalu Rinpoche, Darjeeling
Bokar Rinpoche, Darjeeling
Kanjur Rinpoche, Darjeeling

Tulku Pema Wangyal Rinpoche, Sarnath
H.H. Gyalwa Karmapa, New Delhi
Rinjing Dorje, Kathmandu
Dolpo Wangyal, Kathmandu
Geshe Rabten Rinpoche, Dharamsala
Thubten Zopa Rinpoche, Kathmandu
Thubten Yeshes Rinpoche, Kathmandu
Sogyal Rinpoche, Darjeeling
Tenzing Norgay, Sherpa mountaineer
Sonam Kazi, Darjeeling
Lobsang Lhalungpa, Darjeeling
Lama Jamspal Rinpoche, Sarnath
Sabchu Rinpoche, Kathmandu
Pecham, Kathmandu
Chogyam Trungpa, New Delhi
Kyabje Ling Rinpoche, Dharamsala
Hindu, Burmese, Buddhist Teachers
Mataji, Varanasi
Manavajra Vajracharya, Kathmandu
Yogi Chen Chinese Tibetologist, Kalimpong
Ganesh Baba, Darjeeling
Ramakrishna, Sarnath
Neem Karoli Baba, Nainital
Kirpal Singh, Hardiwar
Shri Anandamoyi Ma, Varanasi
Harish Johari, Bareilly
Munindra Ji vipasanna teacher, Bodh Gaya
Freda Bedi, Karma Ketchog Palmo, abbess,
Tilokpur Tibetan nunnery
U Sumangala, abbot Burmese rest house, Bodh Gaya
Swami A.C. Bhaktivedanta founder Krishna Consciousness,
Vrindavan
Lokesha Chandra, Buddhist iconographer, New Delhi

Annotated Bibliography

During the process of editing *Houseboat on the Ganges & A Room in Kathmandu,* memories of so many friends and teachers sprang to mind. A few are mentioned in the letters and more in the acknowledgements.

This short list of books further explores the community of twentieth century travelers, teachers, and students of Sanskrit, Tibetan, Nepali, tabla, sitar, surbahar, bansuri flute, anthropology, thangka and yantra painting, who began studies of Vajrayana, Mahayana, Hinayana, Vipassana, Hinduism, Dzogchen, Meditation, Yoga, Sanskrit, Tibetan, Nepalese, Ayurveda and Bharatanatyam in the post-beat sixties. Many subsequently wrote books, translated texts, became performers, dharma practitioners, meditation teachers, and founders of nonprofit educational institutions around the world. This list of references and books by acquaintances represents only a fraction of those I knew or knew about who traveled and studied in the sixties.

Traveler's Journals

Allen Ginsberg, *Indian Journals, Notebooks, Diary, Blank Pages, Writings,* Grove Atlantic, 1996.

Gary Snyder, *Passage Through India,* Grey Fox Press, 1972.

Joanne Kyger, *Japan and Indian Journals,* Tombouctou, 1981.

Ram Dass, *Be Here Now,* Lama Foundation, Taos, NM, 1971.

Agehananda Bharati, *The Ochre Robe,* Doubleday, NY. 1970 and *The Tantric Tradition,* Samuel Weiser, 1975. Swami, as I called him, was one of my professors at the University of Washington in 1978.

The Asian Journal of Thomas Merton, New Directions Books, 1973.

In November 1968 three weeks before his untimely death, Thomas Merton, poet, social activist, theologian, mystic and Trappist monk of the Abbey of Gethsemani, met with the reclusive Tibetan *dzogchen* master Chatral Sangye Dorje Rinpoche in his rugged hermitage in Ghoom, West Bengal. "I was profoundly moved, because he is so obviously a great man, a true practitioner of *dzogchen*," Merton wrote. That same month I painted a Tara mandala at Chatral Sangye Dorje Rinpoche's hermitage. As a shy art and calligraphy apprentice in her twenties, to think that I must have crossed paths with Thomas Merton on that rugged mountain trail.

When I met Harold Talbot around that same time in Darjeeling in 1968 during Merton's Asian pilgrimage—and just weeks before Merton's untimely accidental death in Thailand—Harold talked about his work and travels with Merton in India. Harold co-founded Buddhayana Foundation and translates and writes about Tibetan Buddhism.

Scholars, Friends, Acquaintances

Keith Dowman, *Ornaments of Illumination*, Kalimpong, 1970. When we lived in Darjeeling Keith published his first book of translations of Tibetan prayers. I gave him the text of a gnas 'khor or pilgrimage guidebook to Nepal that a Bhutanese lama on pilgrimage gave me in Bodh Gaya. The original text is about the history of the stupa at Boudhanath in Nepal. Keith's translation, *The Legend of the Great Stupa*, was published by Tarthang Tulku's Dharma Publishing in 1973.

William Stablein, *The Mahakalatantra: A Theory of Ritual Blessings and Tantric Medicine*, doctoral dissertation, Columbia University, NY, 1976. William, who arrived in Nepal on a Fulbright Fellowship in 1968, spent four years researching Mahakala. His other book *Healing Image: The Great Black One*, Snow Lion Graphics, 1990, also included his research on the Mahakala tantra.

Rinjing Dorje, *Tales of Uncle Tompa: The Legendary Rascal of Tibet*, Dorje Ling Publishers, San Rafael, Calif., 1975. I wrote an introduction to a later edition of the Uncle Tompa tales illustrated by Addison Smith.

Rinjing was a friend and neighbor in Svayambhunath Nepal in 1971 and later in Seattle where we both settled. A Tibetan storyteller, he also wrote and illustrated the first Tibetan cookbook, *Food in Tibetan Life*, Prospect Books, London, 1986.

Robert Lewis Gross, *The Sadhus of India: A Study of Hindu Asceticism*, Rawat, India, 1992. I met Robert in Darjeeling in 1969 shortly after he arrived to begin research for his Ph.D. His ethnographic account of India's sadhus with whom he lived for four years is a classic in socio-cultural anthropology.

Roger Williams founded a Berkeley, California publishing company, Snow Lion Graphics. When I met Roger in Kathmandu in 1970 he gave me a number of his Tibetan hand-carved woodblock prints on Nepalese lokta paper, some he hand colored, which are in my collection of Tibetan woodblock prints.

Terris Temple, an accomplished Tibetan thangka painter was one of my first acquaintances in 1966 when I lived in the Burmese Buddhist Vihara in Sarnath. Terris studied Tibetan painting for many years and founded Liberation Arts to preserve and restore Tibetan art. http://fineartamerica. com/profiles/terris-temple.html

Lama Anagarika Govinda, *The Way of the White Clouds: A Buddhist in Tibet*, Rider and Company, London, 1966 and *Foundations of Tibetan Mysticism*, London, 1959. Lama Govinda and his wife the artist Li Gotami lived at Kalimat, a house on Crank's Ridge, Almora, owned by the American Tibetan translator W.Y. Evans-Wentz who published important works on Milarepa, Dream Yoga and especially an early edition of *The Tibetan Book of the Dead* in 1927. Where I lived in Orissa, India, one summer, the ruins of Evans-Wentz's meditation hut lent a ghostly ambiance to the farm.

The writings of Alfred Sorenson were collected in *Dancing with the Void: The Innerstandings of a Rare-born Mystic*, edited by Betty Camhi and Gurubaksh Rai, Blue Dove Press, 2001. When I met Sunyata or Sunyabhai as I knew him, a Danish mystic and recluse in 1968, he lived in what he called his "Immortal Garden of Emptiness," at Kalimat on Crank's Ridge, outside of Almora. At 78 years old he was almost sixty years older than I was.

Yogi C.M. Chen, a self-styled Chinese Buddhist pilgrim, scholar and author of many pamphlets he printed to distribute free to spread the teachings of the Buddha. He gave me most of the eighteen pamphlets in my collection that he published between 1963 and 1971. A few of his titles include #32; *The Practice of Pure-Land School Simplified*; # 35 *Milarepa: His Personal Teaching of Renunciation and* # 46 which Keith Dowman and I sponsored, *"A Short Dictionary of Buddhist Hybrid Pali."* He wanted to attract hippie travelers with titles like *#52 Welcome Hippies By This Way* and *#53 Selected Han-Shan Poems for Hippie Reading* which he amusingly credited as being published through a "Gift by The Buddhist Hippies Leader, Ven. Gary Snyder, California, U.S.A." He always included a Letters from Readers section which reads like a humorous Who's Who of many western friends and scholars living in India in the sixties. http://www.yogichen.org/gurulin/gc/gc_e.html

Nik Douglas, *Tibetan Tantric Charms and Amulets: 230 Examples Reproduced from Original Woodblocks*, Dover, NY. 1978. Nik visited William and I in Kathmandu after he returned from the region of Dolpo. He showed us many of the Tibetan woodblock prints of deities, charms, amulets, and prayer flags he collected on his trip and later published.

Gene Smith, a dedicated Field Director of the Library of Congress, microfilmed Tibetan texts in India for twenty-five years. His personal collection of 12,000 Tibetan texts, the world's largest private collection of Tibetan literature, is now housed at a University in Chengdu, China at the Tibetan Buddhist Resource Center (https://en.wikipedia.org/wiki/Tibetan_Buddhist_Resource_Center) where the works are being digitalized for online access.

Nicholas Roerich, (1874-1947) was a Russian archeologist, theosophist, peace activist, painter and writer. I visited his family estate in Naggar, a village in Himachal Pradesh in 1968 where Roerich's son Svetoslav lived with his wife Devika Rani, an Indian film actress. The Roerich Estate is now a museum, the International Roerich Memorial Trust in the Kullu Valley with library and art galleries of paintings and folk art.

http://irmtkullu.com/The older brother George de Roerich was a noted Tibetologist and translator.

Before Johan Reinhard, National Geographic explorer and high-altitude anthropologist, discovered and documented a number of 500-year-old Inca mummies in the Andes mountains of Peru, he completed early work documenting Buddhist pilgrimage sites in Nepal.

Alexander Berzin Tibetan scholar, author, translator, spent 30 years in India studying Tibetan Buddhism. The Buddhist Archives of Dr. Alexander Berzin make available his extensive library through the open-sourced website studybuddhism.com. (https://en.wikipedia.org/wiki/Alexander_Berzin_(scholar))

Tsultrim Allione's, *Women of Wisdom* (Arkana, 1984) describes her ordination in India (during the time I lived there) in the Tibetan Kargyupta tradition. She visited our home in Kathmandu. Her book also contains the first translations of biographies of female saints and yoginis. She founded a retreat center, Tara Mandala, in southern Colorado.

Richard Alpert's (Ram Dass) spiritual guidebook, Be Here Now, (Lama Foundation, New Mexico, 1971), details his transformation from Dr. Richard Alpert to Baba Ram Dass.The book is profusely illustrated with black and white drawings, poetry, mantras, spiritual advice and a Manual for Conscious Being.

Bhagavan Das, *It's Here Now (Are you?) A Spiritual Memoir*, Broadway Books, 1997.Bhagavan Das introduced Richard Alpert to Neem Karoli Baba at his ashram in Nainital where I visited in 1968. Bhagavan's spiritual memoir tracks his sadhu travels around India. He has toured widely performing *bhajan*, Hindu sacred songs.

Harish Johari wrote a number of books on Hinduism including *Tools for Tantra, Chakras, Energy Centers for Transformation* and my favorite about the game he introduced me to at his home in Bareilly, India *Leela: The Ancient Game of Self-knowledge Played by Saints and Sadhus in India.*

Other Books by Marilyn Stablein

NONFICTION

Sleeping in Caves: A Sixties Himalayan Memoir

Climate of Extremes: Landscape and Imagination

FICTION

Vermin: A Traveler's Bestiary

The Census Taker: Tales of a Traveler in India and Nepal

The Monkey Thief

POETRY

Milepost 27

Splitting Hard Ground

Night Travels to Tibet

More Night Travels to Tibet

ART

Bind, Alter, Fold: Artist Books

LIMITED EDITIONS

Phantom Circus

A Pot of Soup

High in the Himalayas

Intrusions in Ice

Ticketless Traveler

CPSIA information can be obtained
at www.ICGtesting.com
Printed in the USA
JSHW041557220520
5839JS00002B/10